D1596751

Once Holy Mountain

Once Holy Mountain

A Biblical and Geographical Analysis of Where Mt. Sinai Is Located

Mark H. Sweberg

WIPF & STOCK · Eugene, Oregon

Wipf & Stock
An Imprint of Wipf and Stock Publishers
199 W. 8th Ave., Suite 3
Eugene, OR 97401

www.wipfandstock.com

PAPERBACK ISBN: 978-1-7252-7757-1
HARDCOVER ISBN: 978-1-7252-7758-8
EBOOK ISBN: 978-1-7252-7759-5

07/23/20

Contents

Acknowledgements

I WANT TO THANK my beloved wife, best friend, and partner for life, Nancy, for her patience and support on this project. Her moral support was unwavering and her reviews of many drafts were precise and invaluable. Her belief in me kept me going always. Without that, this book would not exist.

I also want to thank my dear friend Col.-USAF (Ret.) Al Childers. Al is the most accomplished researcher I have ever known. His help was invaluable as he searched, at my behest, for resources and details that appear in the book. His support was also unwavering and complete. I will always be in Al's debt for his help and friendship.

Introduction

MORE THAN THREE THOUSAND years ago, ten plagues and the exodus re-
defined the relationship between God and the children of Israel. At a time
when the empire of Egypt was near its height, a fugitive prince named
Moses was chosen by God to free the Israelite slaves from bondage. These
freed slaves then followed Moses as he returned to a nondescript mountain
in the vast Sinai desert. At Mt. Sinai, Moses had first been directed by God
to return to Israel to free his people and later received from God the Ten
Commandments with affirmation that the Israelites were God's chosen
people. Moses told the freed slaves they had been chosen to serve as God's
messengers, affirming to the world the one true God and the moral and
ethical codes God expected all his children to obey, not just the Israelites.
This mountain was identified as Mt. Sinai.

The Old Testament provides four of the elements of a story that are
identified as basic to information gathering or problem solving: who, what,
when, and why. The missing element in the biblical story of the exodus is
where this occurred. Where is Mt. Sinai? For centuries, scholars and Bible
experts postulated Mt. Sinai's location as well as the route of the exodus.
Over the past one hundred or so years, both scholars and lay people have
raised questions about the location of Mt. Sinai and challenged the long-
standing postulation of the location of Mt. Sinai in the southern Sinai Peninsula mountains.

Many books and articles propose alternative locations for the Holy
Mountain's site, including some that are not even in the Sinai Peninsula. My
research from exploring the region and literature reviews led me to ponder
why there is an absence of the Bible descriptions in so many of the discussions of location. Most written works about Mt. Sinai do not offer evidence
from the biblical text supporting their conclusions, and those that do often
only cite the Bible in passing.

Introduction

This text holds that the historical accuracy, inerrancy, and authority of the Bible are without question. People inspired by God wrote the Bible. While the book itself is accurate and without error as God is without error, authors who wrote the Bible were influenced by their times, cultures, and understandings during their interpretations of God's inspirations. The Bible was written when knowledge of the world, priorities, and perceptions were much different from those of modern scholars and readers of the Bible. One challenge of understanding the Bible is understanding the circumstances that surrounded its writing.

The Bible is the only ancient record of the existence of Mt. Sinai. The Jewish historian who wrote during the Roman era, Josephus, wrote about Mt. Sinai but this was centuries after events of the book of Exodus took place. Josephus' writings about Mt. Sinai were based on his understanding of the Bible and that of other ancient writers. References in the New Testament are even more distanced in centuries from the events and do not offer definitive evidence one way or the other. The Bible provides information and guidance relative to how ancient people and scribes perceived what was important for future readers. Locations are named; that many have not been archaeologically identified and thus remain unknown is a challenge for any scholar's understanding of what the text is telling us.

This book offers an alternative location where we might find the Holy Mountain based on a number of assessment criteria identified tin Table 1: distance from Egypt and Kadesh-Barnea, support by biblical text and non-biblical references, archaeology, geography and logistics considerations, and other scholarly research.

The first criterion is the Bible. The Bible offer insights and evidence on where the ancient Israelites found Mt. Sinai. We know from the book of Exodus that once freed by Pharaoh the former slaves of Egypt followed Moses to the mountain, where Moses received the Ten Commandments and reaffirmation of God's covenant with the children of the patriarch Abraham. The Bible helps us to follow the Israelites from Egypt to the mountain, which is the first leg of the exodus.

The second criterion is the physical requirements placed on the Israelites as they traveled from Egypt to Mt. Sinai. Based on the time frame of the exodus, during the Middle Bronze Age, this book addresses how fast and how far the multitude of freed slaves traveled each day of the journey and how many days it took to reach the mountain. The route of the exodus to Mt. Sinai will be examined according to the biblical text and those locations identified in the Bible that can be connected to archaeologically identified places today. This is a geographical analysis of the route to and location of Mt. Sinai. As such, it will include analysis of where the Israelites started their trek from, because it is essential to know the start point in order to learn where the end point was.

CRITERIA \\ PROPOSED SITES	Distance from Egypt < 75-120 miles	Distance from Kadesh-Barnea	Supported by Bible text	Supported by archeology	Supported by geography	Supported by non-Biblical references	Supported by logistics considerations	Supported by scholars
Sweberg thesis	Yes	Yes	Yes	Yes	Yes	Yes	Yes	No
Jebel Musa (Hobbs)	No	No	No	Yes	No	Yes	Yes	Yes
Jebel Catherine	No	No	No	Yes	No	Yes	Yes	Yes
Jebel Serbal (Schneller)	No	No	No	Yes	No	Yes	Yes	Yes
Jebel al-Lawz (Whittaker)	No	No	No	No	No	No	No	No
Har Karkom (Anati)	No	Yes	No	No	No	No	No	Yes
Hashem el Tarif (TE Team)	No	Yes	Yes	No	Yes	No	No	Yes
Jebel Halal	No	Yes	No	No	No	No	No	No
Arif el Naka	No	Yes	No	No	No	No	No	No

Table 1: Analysis Results for Mt. Sinai Location

My interest in the location of Mt. Sinai began in the late 1980s when I lived in Egypt and worked in the Sinai Peninsula. I returned in the mid-1990s to live and work in the Sinai Peninsula.

I grew up accepting that Mt. Sinai was to be found in the southern Sinai Peninsula. Today the long-accepted mountain is called Jebel Musa in Arabic, the "Mountain of Moses." When I arrived in Egypt in 1988 I looked forward to the job I was given to do with excitement. I also looked forward to exploring the amazing Sinai Peninsula, as well as seeing for myself Mt. Sinai. I read a lot about Mt. Sinai and learned that scholars had been questioning Jebel Musa being the biblical Mt. Sinai for over a century. I also learned that a number of other sites around and outside the peninsula had been proposed as the true biblical site. I visited Mt. Sinai many times in the first six months I was there and the one thing that struck me was how long it took me to reach Mt. Sinai from Cairo driving a Jeep Grand Wagoneer on the paved roads in the desert. I knew from my Bible studies that the Israelites lead by Moses took approximately forty-five days to reach the mountain. I knew this time frame did not make sense.

After hundreds of hours of research, interviews, and "boots on the ground" exploration, I pieced together the three-dimensional puzzle recognized as Mt. Sinai in the book of Exodus. What I learned offers an alternative location of where more than four billion people of the Abrahamic religions (Judaism, Christianity, and Islam) can find the origin of the Ten Commandments. The focus of my research uses Jewish Bible text.

1

Boots on the Ground

The people quarreled with Moses.
"Give us water to drink," they said; and Moses replied to them,
"Why do you quarrel with me? Why do you try the Lord?"

—EXODUS 17:2

THIS CHAPTER IS INTENDED to provide a sense of what the Sinai Peninsula is like today. Geologically and atmospherically, it has not changed significantly since the time of the Bible. The people who live there have the benefit of modern conveniences; nevertheless, they live lives not as different than their ancestors as would be expected.

The Sinai Peninsula is a harsh and desolate environment to those who do not live there. Although there is water to be found, it is sparse and rare and much of the Sinai is lacking. In the ancient past travelers used only a handful of routes to navigate the desert and those were the routes where early travelers found water. Travelers, especially the Bedouin tribes that make the Sinai their home, simply do not travel along areas lacking in water.

The former Israelite slaves would not have known about the oases outside of Egypt. Moses as a learned shepherd would not lead the Israelites in a straight path to Mt. Sinai when water sources were problematic; he would travel from a known water source to another. As it is, according to the Bible, they still found it difficult to find water and Moses had to appeal to God on several occasions for help.

The Bedouin who inhabit the Sinai Peninsula live not much differently from their ancestors. In the course of my duties from 1988 to 1989, I came in contact with many Bedouin and became friends with three chieftains. The chiefs and their people were as gracious to guests as I had read and heard about. None of the Sinai tribes are wealthy; in fact, the tribes are among the poorest of Bedouins in the Middle East today.

Nevertheless, when I visited I was always invited to a meal and if I did not have time for that I always made time to stay for tea and talk. When I accepted an offer to stay for a meal I was treated as royally as their means allowed and I knew that the simple meal I was served was the very best they had. It was both touching and humbling. I was very interested in how they lived and how they traveled from pasturage to pasturage. Lives of desert dwellers have not changed much over the centuries.

The biggest difference is that ownership of small pickup trucks such as those offered by Toyota, Nissan, and British Bedford now enhances Bedouin lives. These vehicles are simple to operate, hardy, and can be maintained between the family and mechanics in the towns that sprinkle the peninsula. The tribes I became familiar with were small—a few dozen families and their animals, which represented most of their combined wealth. Goats and donkeys are the most important animals, especially the goats that the Bedouin rely on for fur, meat, milk, cheese, and their hides, all of which are used. They travel in family groups at distances entirely based on the needs of the animals. An average travel day starts early in the morning with prayers followed by breakfast, which includes tea and coffee. Bedouin care for the animals while the camp is taken down and loaded into the pickup truck. The truck leaves and arrives at the next stop-over site many hours before the family arrives.

When I asked about the distances traveled, each of the chiefs I came to know gave me pretty much the same answer, around four to seven miles, or six to eleven kilometers. The animals are rarely pushed, as nothing is done to potentially impact their health. One main exception to this is when a sandstorm is imminent. In these cases the family will seek out whatever cover or protection is available and herd the animals into this location to wait out the storm. A long sandstorm can upset the time frame for a day's travels, causing the tribe to seek another, closer, overnight location. If one is available, the chief will use another modern convenience, his cell phone, to call his people with the truck to relocate to the new campsite.

After I visited the Mt. Sinai location in the southern region of the peninsula, I started questioning its legitimacy as the Holy Mountain. At the time I was an active-duty Army officer and my interest was passing. When I next returned to Egypt and the Sinai in the mid-1990s, I had retired from the Army and my interest was greater as I read many books and articles about Mt. Sinai in anticipation of my return to the region. By this time I had discovered that the biblical text played almost no role in other claims for Mt. Sinai. During this second time working in the Sinai Peninsula, I spent much of my off-time exploring the other locations advocated by scholars as the site of Mt. Sinai and started to develop my own theories. A few years ago I determined to pool my research and present my own work on the location of Mt. Sinai and this book is the result of that effort.

2

Defining an Approach to Mt. Sinai

"Thus says the Lord, the God of Israel: Let My people go that they may celebrate a festival for Me in the Wilderness." But pharaoh said, "Who is the Lord
that I should heed Him and let Israel go? I do not know the Lord, nor will I
let Israel go." They [Moses and Aaron] answered, "The God of the Hebrews
has manifested Himself to us. Let us go, we pray, a distance of *three days
into the wilderness* to sacrifice to the Lord our God, lest He strike us with
pestilence or sword." But the king of Egypt said to them, "Moses and Aaron,
why do you distract the people from their tasks? Get to your labors!"

—EXODUS 5:1–4 (EMPHASIS ADDED)

MT. SINAI EVOKES POWERFUL images to anyone of the Jewish or Christian
faith. Although Mt. Sinai appears in the Islamic faith's Qur'an, it does not
have the impact it does on Christians and Jews. For many people the exodus and Mt. Sinai evoke images influenced by the wonderful motion picture produced by Cecil B. Demille, *The Ten Commandments*. Even though
Demille did not accurately portray the exodus according to the Bible, the
visual images of Mt. Sinai portrayed in the movie are forever burned in our
memory. Christians and Jews who went to Sunday school, read the Bible, or
studied the Bible are familiar with the story.

As the second book of the Old Testament (the Tanakh), the book of
Exodus recalls the most seminal event in the history of the Abrahamic

religions. The story of God's decision to use his most important prophet, Moses, to get the pharaoh of Egypt to free the Israelites and then subsequently bestow upon these people his Ten Commandments at Mt. Sinai is well known.

Jews celebrate the story annually during the second most holy day on the Jewish calendar, Passover. In our modern, "enlightened" world, the story of the exodus is, for many people, just that—a story. But for many it is much, much more. The Bible is not a book of stories and homilies. The Bible is the first book of its kind in history. It is a written history of the family of the first patriarch, Abraham, and the people who originated from him and his descendants. Until the Bible, no other written work that has been discovered was created as a factual history.

Written works from the great kingdoms of Egypt were created to help explain the gods to the people and how the gods were to be propitiated, or to glorify the reigning pharaoh. Earlier works that have been discovered among the ruins of Sumer, Assyria, Babylon, and other ancient kingdoms were written to reflect economic transactions or teach heroic stories about the ancient gods and great heroes, such as Gilgamesh. These were not histories; they had a different purpose. They were never written to reflect factual accounts of people or nations. The Bible was the first. What also makes the Bible unique is that the one true God whom the children of Israel believed in took a personal hand in the Bible's creation. God did not write the book; he inspired the writers who did.

The location of biblical Mt. Sinai has long been held to be a specific location among the mountains located in the southern Sinai Peninsula. Today called Mt. Musa locally, this site was without question for centuries. Beginning in the nineteenth century, however, higher criticism of the Bible led to questioning the text of the Bible, the historicity of the Bible itself, and its reliability. The site of Mt. Sinai also came under fire by critics challenging its location and the basis for its historical role in the exodus, indeed if the exodus even occurred.

The Bible offers very little description of Mt. Sinai itself. What is said indicates the mountain was nondescript, leading us to believe it was not the most imposing mountain in the Sinai Peninsula or the tallest. In fact, about the only assumption that can be derived from the biblical text about Mt. Sinai is that it was important and significant only during the time in exodus when God made his presence known there. God manifested his presence on the mountain to meet with Moses and later to talk with Moses and instruct him, as well as his brother, Aaron, as they prepared to meet with the pharaoh to free the Israelite slaves.

Later in Exodus the mountain earned brief importance, and holiness, as the Israelites encamped at its base so Moses could receive the Ten Commandments, or the *Aseret Hadeverim* (Hebrew for "The Ten Sayings" or "The Ten Matters"), from God. Once the Israelites traveled away from the mountain on their forty-year sojourn in the desert, written references to Mt. Sinai slipped into oblivion and it lost its importance as a holy site. It reemerged only briefly in 1 Kings 19:8, when the prophet Elijah took refuge in a cave on Mt. Sinai, but 1 Kings makes no mention of the mountain being holy. It was the Once Holy Mountain and nothing more.

There has long been a belief among Jewish rabbis and ancient Jewish sages that descriptions in the Bible are intentionally scant and make it challenging to find support for the location of the Holy Mountain because it was never intended that Mt. Sinai would become a place of lasting importance.

Among the foremost of early Jewish sages, Rashi, who lived in eleventh-century France (1040–1105), and Maimonides, who lived in twelfth-century Egypt (1135–1204), wrote that God intentionally selected Mt. Sinai because it was "humble," unprepossessing, compared to other mountains.[1] The logic of this is based on the understanding that if the location of Mt. Sinai were known it would become a place of pilgrimage and the message of the exodus, the Ten Commandments, and the covenant with God would all be lost.[2]

Early Jews interpreted the passage in Exodus 19:12, "Beware of going up the mountain or touching the border of it. Whoever touches the mountain shall be put to death," as a clear indication that God did not want the mountain's location to be known. He did not want the Israelites following Moses to approach the mountain and he did not want future generations to even know its location. This is also possibly why the mountain was nondescript.

Yet to many believers of the Bible the site of Mt. Sinai holds great fascination and the search for Mt. Sinai may never end. There are currently at least ten sites in and around the Sinai Peninsula with adherents supporting them as the true site of the Holy Mountain. Figure 1 depicts seven of these locations. There may be more; this map reflects only those sites that have or had adherents who wrote books or articles favoring them.

In addition to the dearth of biblical information on Mt. Sinai, there are no other ancient documents to help scholars seeking its location; the Bible is the only source document for Mt. Sinai. Archaeology has offered some clues by uncovering places that may have been along the route traveled by the Israelites en route to the Holy Mountain from Egypt. But here too the evidence is sparse and many places listed in the Bible as being along the path have not yet been found and may never be discovered.

For all the lack of extant evidence, the biblical text offers clues that can narrow the area in which the Holy Mountain is located. These clues and the conclusions we can derive from them are what this book is about.

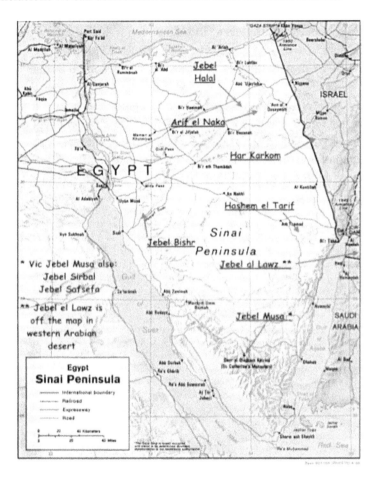

Figure 1: Map of Sinai annotated with the locations of the more prominent mountains that have been proposed as the true Mt. Sinai (discussed later in this book). Image available from a number of websites, including www.vidiani.com/detailed-relief-map-of-egypt-sinai-peninsula-with-roads/ and mapsof.net/egypt/sinai-peninsula-map.

One approach to finding the site of biblical Mt. Sinai begins in understanding some aspects of the travels of the host of freed Israelites. The search for Mt. Sinai is an exercise in understanding geography and logistics. To narrow the search for the mountain's location, five questions need to be addressed: Where did the Exodus start? Where did the host of freed slaves depart from Egypt? How long did the journey last before they arrived at the base of Mt. Sinai? How far did the Israelite people travel each day? What was the route of travel? We have to ascertain the conditions and the resultant average rate of travel that would have been possible for a large number of people: healthy, aged, and toddlers, and including the animals they brought with them. How many people left Egypt with Moses?

The Bible provides names of places that were along the route of the Exodus and archaeology has identified candidates for some of these locations, some of which are key, while geographic descriptions from the biblical text offer evidence for other locations. How close to Egypt did the mountain have to be to meet time lines outlined in the Bible?

In all of this the Bible offers clues. Understanding the clues helps us to narrow the range of geography wherein the search for Sinai needs to be focused.

3

Where Else Has Mt. Sinai Been Posited?

For when the horses of pharaoh with his chariots and his horsemen went
into the sea, the LORD brought back the waters of the sea upon them, but the
people of Israel walked on dry ground in the midst of the sea.

—EXODUS 15:19

RESEARCH BEGINS WITH THE beginning. In this case, the Bible offers
that Moses left from a part of Egypt where the sea could be parted so the
Israelites could flee into the desert and be forever free of Egypt.

Traditionalists and historians believed for centuries that Mt. Sinai is
located in the mountain-ous region in the south-ern tip of the Sinai Peninsula. Today the mountain is called Mt. Moses or Jebel Musa. This was the accepted location for the Holy Mountain for centuries starting around the second century of the Common Era. It has been joined by a number of contenders and in the

Figure 2: Photo of Jebel Musa, taken by the author
in 1989 when exploring the terrain believed for
centuries to be Mt. Sinai.

past century over half a dozen peaks have been declared the true Mt. Sinai. There are still many people, both scholars and lay people, that remain convinced that the original contender for the true Mt. Sinai remains Jebel Musa. Figure 2 is a contemporary view of Jebel Musa.

The other sites for Mt. Sinai lie in widely separate areas and some are not in the Sinai Peninsula. One site that is close is another mountain about twenty miles from Jebel Musa. The mountain is Jebel Serbal and at one time believers in this mountain contended it was a more legitimate Mt. Sinai than Jebel Musa or other mountains. Beyond the Sinai Peninsula is a site among the extinct volcanoes in the northwest Arabian Desert called Jebel al-Lawz.

Another peak proposed is located not far from Kadesh Barnea, near the city of Beersheba in modern Israel, called Har Karkom. More recently some scholars have offered the mountain Hashem el-Tarif, close to Bir Taba and the southeastern Egyptian border with Israel, as the possible site of Mt. Sinai. There are articles published making a case for two mountains located in the northeastern part of the Sinai Peninsula, Jebel Halal and Arif el Naka.

This chapter reviews some of these contenders, marked in Figure 1.

Table 1 (shown again below for convenience) organizes by way of a graphic overview the results of analysis of all the potential contenders for being biblical Mt. Sinai. The vertical axis lists potential sites while assessment criteria are listed along the horizontal axis. This author chose the following criteria to determine a most obvious Mt. Sinai location: distance from Egypt and Kadesh-Barnea, reliable biblical and nonbiblical reference, archeological and geographic support, logistical considerations, and consideration of other scholarly inputs. Conclusions whether each site meets the criteria are identified across the table. Each site will be discussed in the remainder of this book except for three sites lacking in scholarly support: Jebel al-Lawz, Jebel Halal and Arif el Naka.

CRITERIA / PROPOSED SITES	Distance from Egypt < 75-120 miles	Distance from Kadesh-Barnea	Supported by Bible text	Supported by archeology	Supported by geography	Supported by non-Biblical references	Supported by logistics considerations	Supported by scholars
Sweberg thesis	Yes	Yes	Yes	Yes	Yes	Yes	Yes	No
Jebel Musa (Hobbs)	No	No	No	Yes	No	Yes	Yes	Yes
Jebel Catherine	No	No	No	Yes	No	Yes	Yes	Yes
Jebel Serbal (Schneller)	No	No	No	Yes	No	Yes	Yes	Yes
Jebel al-Lawz (Whittaker)	No	No	No	No	No	No	No	No
Har Karkom (Anati)	No	Yes	No	No	No	No	No	Yes
Hashem el Tarif (TE Team)	No	Yes	Yes	No	Yes	No	No	Yes
Jebel Halal	No	Yes	No	No	No	No	No	No
Arif el Naka	No	Yes	No	No	No	No	No	No

Table 1: Analysis Results for Mt. Sinai Location

The proposed site of Jebel al-Lawz has been automatically dismissed for several reasons. This location in the Arabian Desert of Saudi Arabia is so far away from the eastern border of Egypt that it has to be eliminated. A large host of people and animals the size and condition of the fleeing Israelites could not have crossed the desert or been supported by oases locations to reach the distance in the limited time described in the Bible. The rate of travel and size of the host following Moses will be discussed further later on. Dr. Charles Whittaker, a strong advocate for Jebel al-Lawz, contends the Israelites would have traveled around twenty miles per day or more during the Exodus. This is a speed far in excess of reality. And most relevantly, Jebel al-Lawz is not located in the Sinai Peninsula. The Bible makes it clear that the Holy Mountain was in the Sinai Peninsula.

Another site eliminated after careful analysis is Har Karkom. This site is favored by esteemed archaeologist Emmanuel Anati, who wrote a beautiful book about this mountain titled *The Mountain of God: Har Karkom*. Anati presents in his book a large amount of evidence for the archaeological history of the mountain, but he spends almost no time on the biblical connections surrounding Har Karkom. This is the major flaw in Anati's book and the theory that Har Karkom is Mt. Sinai.

Har Karkom is physically located around thirty-five kilometers inside the boundaries of the Promised Land as described in the Bible. According to Genesis 15:18, God promised Abraham, "this land, from the River of Egypt to the great river, the river Euphrates." The River of Egypt has long been accepted to mean wadi El-Arish, which today runs south from the town of El-Arish along the western border of Israel. The biblical text records that the Israelites would wander forty years in the wilderness *before* entering the Promised Land. If Har Karkom were biblical Mt. Sinai, it would place the Holy Mountain inside the borders of the Promised Land. For no other reason than this, Har Karkom is not a viable contender for biblical Mt. Sinai.

Related to Mt. Sinai being inside the boundaries of the Promised Land, if Har Karkom was Mt. Sinai Moses would have been able to walk the Promised Land from this location rather than wait until his final days to view the land from Mt. Nebo in present-day western Jordan. God denied Moses the privilege of entering the Promised Land but granted him a view of the land from Mt. Nebo only shortly before God took Moses to heaven.

Two additional sites have also been eliminated after diligent research and a lack of scholarly support. On the map they are Jebel Halal and Arif el Naka. Both are located in or near wadi El-Arish in the northeast part of the Sinai. Both are also located close to east-west routes along the main part of the Sinai used by travelers going between Egypt and Canaan. These sites would have placed Mt. Sinai in much too well-traveled areas and specifically in areas that God told Moses he would lead the Israelites away from for reason of potential threats.

4

Starting Point for the Exodus

You go free on this day, in the month of Abib.

—EXODUS 13:4

EXODUS 13:4 IS IMPORTANT in describing the departing point for the Exodus. It provides the *when* and *why* of timing of the march to Mt. Sinai. The starting point is key to determining the distance of Mt. Sinai from Egypt as assessed in Table 1. The month of Abib on the ancient Hebrew calendar corresponds to late March and early April—springtime. In the spring, God brought the people out of Egypt, when travel would be best as the climate had not yet become hot, was past being cold, and there was a period with little rain. The Israelites took their first steps toward Mt. Sinai when and where travel was easiest.

As with any adventure or trip, the Exodus began with the first step. In this case, that first step depended upon where Moses met with pharaoh after God charged Moses to free the Israelites. This was the location from where the Exodus began as pharaoh granted freedom for the slaves after the tenth plague and gave his decision to Moses.

The search for the starting point (the *where*) begins long before the story of the Book of Exodus. It begins in the first book of the Bible, the book of Genesis. In this book the Bible records how the Israelites first settled in Egypt, in the land of Goshen, in the northeast part of the Nile Delta. When the patriarch Joseph prospered in Egypt after pharaoh elevated him to the second-most powerful position after pharaoh, he helped his family also to settle in Egypt (Genesis 45–46).

The Bible records how Joseph came to be in Egypt as a slave and through a series of circumstances rose to prominence and power after setting up a program of grain preservation that prevented the kingdom from suffering from a seven-year famine. With his elevation, Joseph settled in Egypt's capital, where he remained in proximity to pharaoh and continued to contribute to Egypt's prosperity. As will be discussed later, this capital would have been Avaris, located in the eastern Nile Delta.

In the biblical story Joseph's family, recorded in the book of Genesis, whom he had not seen in many years, came to Egypt from Canaan fleeing a devastating drought. After reuniting with Joseph, the family was given a fertile tract of land by pharaoh to live on. According to Genesis, pharaoh gave Joseph and his family the "best part of the land "(Egypt); (pharaoh) let them stay in the region of Goshen" (Gen 47:6).

The text of the Bible infers that Goshen was located in the northeastern Nile Delta. Since Avaris was also located in the eastern Nile Delta, Joseph was thus residing in close proximity to where pharaoh lived and ruled. It was in this region of the northeastern Nile Delta that they settled and built their lives among their Egyptian neighbors. As the Israelites migrated to Egypt and settled, they "multiplied and increased very greatly" (Exod 1:7). Over time, these Israelite settlers spread out and found prosperity and acceptance throughout the land of Egypt.

Figure 3 offers the probable location of Avaris, which today is Tell el-Dab'a, in the northeast region of the Nile Delta. This is the most likely location for the city accepted today by most Egyptologists.[3] The map also identifies Avaris as the site of Ra'amses (Rameses). In this the map is not correct. Rameses was a region in the eastern Nile Delta that included the area of Goshen. It was also a store city near Avaris, which has caused confusion as scribes and ancient scholars have blurred the distinctions between Rameses the store city and Rameses the eastern Nile Delta region. This will be discussed later.

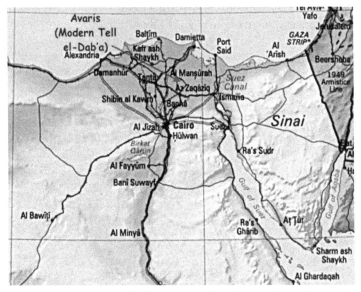

Figure 3: Map showing probable location of Avaris at modern archaeological excavation Tell el-Dab'a.

The pharaohs of ancient Egypt ruled from one of four capital cities. In the Nile Delta, Avaris was the capital of the Hyksos pharaohs of the Seventeenth Dynasty. Figure 4 shows the locations of the other capitals: Memphis, Thebes, and El-Amarna. Each city served at one time or another as the capital of one or more of ancient Egypt's pharaonic dynasties or individual pharaohs.

After living for many years in harmony with their Egyptian neighbors, the descendants of Joseph and his family had a change in fortune. The Bible records that a new king arose in Egypt who "did not know Joseph" (Exod 1:8) and who was fearful of the numerous Israelites. This king enslaved the Israelites and put them to work as forced labor (Exod 1:8–11). The new king was Ahmose I, who defeated and removed the Hyksos rulers from Egypt.

The Hyksos were non-Egyptians who entered Egypt from the Near East and defeated the Egyptians to establish their dynasty in the eastern Nile Delta of Egypt. This took place around 1650 BCE. Southern Egypt remained in the hands of the Egyptian Sixteenth Dynasty with its capital in Thebes, present-day Luxor. These two kingdoms coexisted relatively peacefully until around 1550 BCE, when Egyptian Pharaoh Ahmos I defeated and expelled the Hyksos and reunited Upper and Lower Egypt and established the Eighteenth Dynasty over all of Egypt.

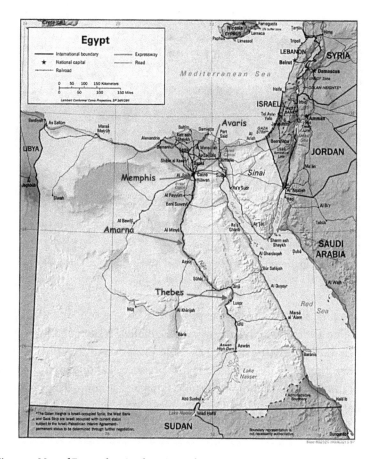

Figure 4: Map of Egypt showing locations of Amarna, Memphis, Avaris and Thebes.

A case can be made that, being outsiders themselves, the Hyksos would have been more tolerant of other outsiders coming into Egypt and that is why they not only allowed Joseph's family to settle in Egypt, but the Hyksos pharaoh allowed Joseph to have so much power. When Pharaoh Ahmos I reunited Egypt he would not have known or would not have cared about the history of the people or of Joseph's warm relationships with the northern rulers. To the new rulers these people were foreigners who posed an internal threat because of their growing numbers and influence. So the new rulers enslaved the people.

The slaves built the store cities of Pithom and Rameses for pharaoh (Exod 1:12). Rameses is recorded in the Bible as the city from which the Israelites left Egypt. Some scholars critical of the Bible's historicity have argued that Rameses was the name of a much later pharaoh and could not have been the name of the site from where the Israelites departed. Additionally, it is difficult to accept that a store city would have been where pharaoh was and where he met with Moses when Moses came to him asking that the Israelite slaves be set free.

However, there are several reasons for Rameses being in the biblical text during this time before the Exodus. One is that a scribe at a later date could have been allowed, or was inspired by God, to change the text to reflect this later name. It would have been more familiar to the people in later centuries studying or reading from the biblical text. Another reason could be that the name Rameses was an already accepted regional name in use at the time.

While either reason is plausible, the second reason is more so. Long before any Rameses ruled as pharaoh, the land of Goshen was a district of Rameses.[4] This is the same area of the northeastern delta that was originally settled by the descendants of those people who came to Egypt at the invitation of Joseph. This was where pharaohs and the nobility of Egypt built summer palaces to retreat to in the summer, taking advantage of the more moderate temperatures in the delta. Moses was born near one of these palaces and as a baby was placed by his mother into a waterproof wicker basket and set into the waters of the Nile. He drifted with the current as his sister watched from the shore to see what would "befall him" (Exod 2:4). He was found soon after by the "daughter of pharaoh" (Exod 2:3). She lived in one of these palaces close to where Moses was born. The princess made him her son and named him Moses because she "drew him out of the water" (Exod 2:10). Once Moses was placed in the royal family by his stepmother, the "daughter of Pharaoh," he would have been raised as a royal son.

Moses' birth family would have resided near this pharaoh's palace, where they had lived since before Moses' birth, which answers the question where Moses traveled to when he traveled back and forth from Mt. Sinai to visit his kin (Exod 4:18). This back and forth is very important to the narrative explaining where Mt. Sinai must be. This will be discussed in more detail later when the book discusses the proximate location of Mt. Sinai in respect to Egypt's borders. Moses' family lived in the same delta region identified as Rameses and settled by Joseph and his family. Again, this is consistent with where the majority of the Israelites lived before and during their captivity. Today, as noted earlier, many Egyptologists have accepted the excavations of Tell el-Dab'a as the site of Avaris. This was also the western terminus of a principle travel route from Canaan to Egypt and beyond, via the Way of the Philistines or, as it was known to the ancient Egyptians, the Way of Horus, which ran along the Mediterranean coast to Gaza (see Figure 5).

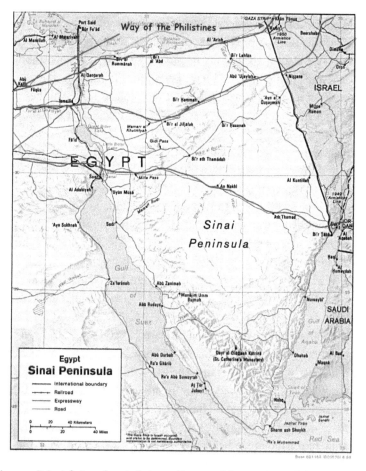

Figure 5: Principle travel route between Egypt and Canaan, Way of the Philistines, which was known to ancient Egypt as the Way of Horus.

This is the area where Moses met with pharaoh and where the Exodus started. Perhaps not Avaris, but from one of the palaces in the northeastern delta region of Rameses, which included the lands of Goshen, granted by pharaoh to Joseph as reward for Joseph saving the country from years of famine (as narrated in Gen 41:1–57). The evidence of this is in the Bible. Although not explained in a straightforward manner, nevertheless, the evidence from the biblical text supports the ties that link Moses with Joseph and where the Israelite people settled in Egypt.

5

The Hyksos

Now there arose a new king over Egypt. He knew nothing about Yosef but said to his people, "Look, the descendants of Israel have become a people too numerous and powerful for us. Come, let's use wisdom in dealing with them. Otherwise, they'll continue to multiply; and in the event of war they might ally themselves with our enemies, fight against us and leave the land altogether." So they put slavemasters over them to oppress them with forced labor, and they built for pharaoh the storage cities of Pitom and Ra'amses.

—EXODUS 1:8–11

ANOTHER KEY CONSIDERATION SUPPORTING the assessment criteria in Table 1 is in understanding the condition of the Israelite slaves before the Exodus began. This chapter addresses both the presumed starting point and logistics considerations that would control the distance this mass of people and animals could travel.

Before moving to the next step in identifying the location for Mt. Sinai, it is worth a digression to consider the Bible's description of the Hyksos rulers of Egypt. Had this dynasty not ruled Egypt when it did, the history of the Israelite peoples, the family of Abraham, and the giving of the Ten Commandments may have taken a very different path.

The Hyksos were important to the Exodus narrative because they were tolerant of foreigners; they allowed immigration and settlement, particularly by people from Canaan seeking escape from environmental crisis.

This in turn enabled Joseph to rise in power to become the second-most powerful man in the empire after pharaoh. The Hyksos evidently rewarded ability and skill. This was unlike all the great and not-so-great dynasties that ruled ancient Egypt before and after the Hyksos who were not tolerant of foreigners. Ahmose I went to war with the Hyksos kingdom, defeated it, and reunited Upper and Lower Egypt, establishing the Eighteenth Dynasty. Having removed a foreign ruling class from Egypt, the new pharaoh was suspicious of non-native Egyptians and particularly suspicious of the large population of Israelites residing among the population. Ahmose I saw this population as a potential threat and thereby enslaved them.

The Hyksos were a foreign dynasty that ruled Egypt around 1700–1500 BCE, depending on which dating protocol is accepted. They were "Asiatics" who came from somewhere in the Ancient Near East. Where they originated, how they came to conquer the rulers of northern Egypt, and how they managed to establish their dynasty in the Nile Delta area are not known. There are theories but no definitive proofs. Even the meaning of the term "Hyksos" which we use to describe them is a point of discussion among scholars, but it is generally accepted to mean "of Asiatic origin."[5]

Note that the term "Asiatic" had a different connotation when the Hyksos ruled. Today it would infer people from Asia, but in that period Asiatics, to Egyptians, were people from Canaan and lands to the east of Canaan, such as Syria-Palestine. Prior to the establishment of the Hyksos dynasty, there is evidence that Asiatics or foreigners had settled in Egypt with no resistance from either the Egyptian populace or the rulers.

It is difficult to find records dating to the early Egyptian dynasties much before the Twelfth. There are records on papyri and stele starting around the Twelfth Dynasty, from the time of Amenemhat I, approximately 1990–1800 BCE, to the rule of Sobekhotep, around approximately 1800–1650 BCE, recording "many Asiatics who worked for Egyptian masters." Many of these foreigners had their names changed to Egyptian names, which was common at the time.[6]

Asiatics entered Egypt for a variety of reasons. Some came from Canaan during droughts or famines and opted to remain. Others came as prisoners of war who later won their freedom and many were born of Asiatic parents who resided in Egypt. From the evidence, these people found work in the Egyptian agricultural fields, as domestic servants, and even as workers in the Egyptian temples. It is clear from these recordings that foreigners were welcome, especially those with skills that benefitted Egyptian society.

Much of this evidence comes from uncovered stele, such as one found in Abydos belonging to an overseer. On the stele are preserved seventeen figures of men and women, and among these are three figures designated as *Aamu*, foreigners, which include a brewer, a female miller, and an un-identified worker.[7] In the city of Abydos as in other locations, steles have been found that were set up by Asiatics in the Egyptian traditions. There are other accounts in papyri and stele showing that the Egyptians were sympathetic towards people coming to Egypt fleeing strife, meteorological disasters, drought, or famine. The result of all this immigration was a rich mix of foreigners living and prospering in Egypt.

The Hyksos ruled Lower Egypt—that is, Egypt from the Nile Delta to the First Cataract—from about 1650 BCE to about 1550 BCE. Asiatics were immigrating into Egypt, mostly in the delta area, starting around 1800 BCE. The Fourteenth Dynasty, Canaanite, emerged in control of the eastern delta and, for a while, coexisted with the Egyptian Thirteenth Dynasty. Around 1650 BCE the Hyksos took control of the entire delta and established the Fifteenth Dynasty. With the collapse of the Egyptian Thirteenth Dynasty, the Egyptian Sixteenth Dynasty was founded, ruling Upper Egypt from its capitol in Thebes.

By the time Ahmose I finally defeated the Hyksos and reunited Egypt, the Asiatics in the delta had established deep roots in the country. The new rulers reduced these people to slavery and set the stage for the Exodus to come and all that came after that.

So the Hyksos rulers of Egypt are important to the Exodus narrative because they were tolerant to foreigners. They were the only Egyptian dynasty that would have enabled Joseph to rise to such heights within the government. Joseph, as the Bible records, was asked to interpret pharaoh's dream. He accurately explained the dream meant that Egypt was about to face seven years of plenty and then would face seven years of famine. Joseph suggested some good sound plans for the kingdom to prepare for the seven bad years and pharaoh appointed him second in command so he could direct and manage the plans. All went well and Egypt continued to prosper.

But as with all things, change happened. And the downfall of the Hyksos and return of an Egyptian dynasty helps to, if not date, narrow the time frame when the Israelites became slaves. Only the Hyksos dynasty could have allowed for Joseph's rise to power during the early to middle Bronze Age, when the Fifteenth Dynasty ruled the Delta. This is the time frame that is consistent with scholarly conjecture about when the time of slavery took place. History would have played out differently had the Hyksos not risen in Egypt.

Although the Hyksos rulers were tolerant of foreigners—which is not to say the Egyptian rulers before or after were not as welcoming to a point—other rulers may not have been inclined to raise up a foreigner to an exalted position as was the case of Joseph. There was a tolerance of foreigners entering Egypt, especially during times of famine or drought. Since early in the history of the Egyptian state, outside groups were known to seek relief and once periods of drought or famine ended these groups often returned to their own lands, though it was just as possible for them to settle in Egypt. One papyrus discovered dating to the Middle Kingdom, the *Prophecy of Neferti*, records refugees from drought in the north outside Egypt came seeking water for themselves and their flocks. A border guard recorded another evidence of this tolerance during the rule of Merenptah, allowing the passage of a large group of herders to obtain water for the herds and the herders. There are other records that support the tolerant policies of a range of pharaohs allowing foreigners to obtain help and support from Egypt.

6

How Long It Took the Israelites
to Reach Mt. Sinai

On the third new moon after the Israelites had gone forth from the land of
Egypt, on that very day, they entered the Wilderness of Sinai. Having journeyed from Rephidim, they entered the wilderness of Sinai and encamped in
the wilderness, Israel encamped there in front of the mountain.

—EXODUS 19:1–2

THE BIBLE DESCRIBES THE length of time for the journey from Egypt to Mt.
Sinai. Foremost in understanding the time line is having a sense of how this
large group of people, including young, old, sick, healthy, pregnant, and
also livestock, traveled. Second is to appreciate what is involved in walking
through the land and terrain of the Sinai Peninsula. This chapter further
provides background for assessing the logistics issues of travel as identified
in Table 1.

The Israelites left Egypt in a hurry. As it is noted in Exodus 12:34, "So
the people took their dough before it was leavened, there kneading bowls
wrapped in their cloaks upon their shoulders." They took what they could
carry or hurriedly load onto donkeys, carts, and whatever else they could
take with them.

Men and women of all ages wore sandals made by slaves and intended
for life in their Egyptian surroundings. They were not designed for long

marches and trekking through deserts, and likely fell apart after a few miles. Their clothes were also homemade, of rough cloth, and they had cloth shawls for their heads to protect from the sun. The people of the Exodus walked. There were no carts for people to ride in, except for the very old, infirm, and small children, because any conveyances were filled with food, tents, and cooking supplies. The rest of their belongings had to be carried on their backs while sticks were used as canes for support and beating the livestock to herd forward and keep from straying.

This mass of people and livestock stretched for miles so that when the front of the march stopped to camp each night, it took hours for the entire mass to halt in place, pasture their animals, and set up their campsites. Each morning, those designated to begin the day's trek began moving forward again, followed by the rest in their order until the last Israelites began again. Each day began an hours-long process of stopping and starting that had to be coordinated so everyone would understand what was happening—over and over again.

The first part of the march was the easiest. Egypt up to the wilderness had for centuries been tamed by civilization. Roads by ancient standards existed. Fields of cotton and rice spread across acres and acres. Probably the biggest challenge initially was not trampling through the pharaoh's fields and destroying whatever was growing in them.

Once the Israelites entered the wilderness and prior to arriving at the Sea of Reeds, they were confronted with rougher conditions: sand, sharp rocks underfoot, the sun beating down, and always the ever-present fear that water and pasturage would not be found in time.

From this author's own experiences, marching through the desert is no simple task. In some cases, the solid-packed sand jolts tired and un-trained joints, especially old joints, while in other areas the sand is deep, causing one to struggle in raising and lowering one's legs to persist forward. The desert is not flat; it is a series of hills and dunes where the horizon can stretch seemingly forever. At some points one can see mountains in the dis-tance without knowing for sure how far away they really are. And travelers understand that there is water either in the form of wells or large oases that cannot be seen until they are almost in front of them. Sometimes the air was heavy with no breeze while at others the air flowed hot, either slowing their pace or pushing them along to a point of exhaustion. In the Sinai and in almost every desert on Earth there are sandstorms. The Israelites would have faced these as well.

Each day in this desert environment, wanderers dug into the land to pitch tents, set up campfires, and stake out animals. The fortunate slept inside on some type of bedding while others fended for themselves under the stars. The next morning, everything was torn down and reloaded onto carts or directly onto the backs of humans and animals, to be carried to the next campsite.

As they approached Mt. Sinai, the ground became increasingly hard, rocky, and uphill.

The Bible also offers some good clues to help determine how long the Israelites traveled from Egypt to Mt. Sinai. According to the text of Exodus 13:4, the Israelites departed from Egypt on the day of the new moon in the month of Abib. They arrived at the Wilderness of Sinai on the first day of the third month (Exod 19:1). The Israelites followed a lunar calendar with each month having thirty days. The new moon of Abib was the fifteenth day of the month.

That the Israelites began their Exodus on the fifteenth day of the month is further corroborated in Numbers 33:3, where the text records, "They set out from Rameses in the first month, on the fifteenth day of the month."

After the departure, the remainder of the month would have been fifteen days. They traveled all of the next month, so thirty days are added to the fifteen for a total of forty-five days. They arrived at the foot of Mt. Sinai the next day, which can mean they took a total of forty-six days to reach the Holy Mountain, but it did not take a full day to arrive so we can settle on a journey of forty-five days total. Additional text affirms the journey took a total of forty-five days. Exodus 16:1 says the Israelites arrived in the Wilderness of Sin on the fifteenth day of the second month. This means it took thirty days to reach the Wilderness of Sin. From here an additional fifteen days were consumed before arriving at Mt. Sinai. Recalling that the host of freed slaves left Egypt on the fifteenth day of the first month, this text supports the position that the total time of the journey was forty-five days: fifteen days of the first month, thirty days of the second month, and arriving on the first day of the third month.

The Israelites traveled from the Wilderness of Sin to Dophkah, from Dophkah to Alush, from Alush to Rephidim, and finally to the Wilderness of Sinai. Rephidim was the last stop before the Israelites arrived in the Wilderness of Sinai according to the text of Numbers 33:15, "They set out from Rephidim and encamped in the Wilderness of Sinai." The biblical text says the Israelites encamped at each of these places and then traveled on. There is nothing to indicate the length of each encampment but the total time it took to reach the Wilderness of Sinai from the Wilderness of Sin was fifteen days, with each encampment lasting only the overnight time to rest before continuing the journey the next morning.

There is one exception; an additional event occurred at Rephidim and before the arrival at Sinai. This was when Amalek "came and fought with Israel" (Exod 17:8). The Amalekites were marauding nomads who attacked the vanguard of the marching Israelites. This was a "surprise attack" (Deut 25:18) that lasted a short time but probably added a day to the overall journey. Exodus 17:8 recounts how the Amalekites "came and fought with Israel at Rephidim." The Israelites were at Rephidim. In the next sentence, Exodus 17:9, Moses tells Joshua, "Tomorrow I will station myself on the top of the hill." Moses does this to inspire the people to prevail over the Amalekites. The battle ended at sunset (Exod 17:12) and the journey to Mt. Sinai concluded the next day.

Biblical experts speculate as to how long the Israelites stopped before crossing the Sea of Reeds: whether for more than a night as Moses awaited God's guidance on how they would circumvent this obstacle, or just one night. When pharaoh arrived, God parted the waters, allowing the Israelites to cross, and their journey continued. Minimum delay likely occurred in the continuation of the journey and only one night was spent encamped before the arrival of pharaoh.

The Israelites did not travel nonstop for forty-five days, nor did they travel via a direct route. In the desert there is no such thing as a direct route, and Sinai is, indeed, a desert. The Israelites would have followed an irregular route that would have brought them to water and grasses, or pasturage, for their animals. In fact, at the beginning of the journey after the Israelites encamped at Etham, God told Moses to turn back and encamp at Pi-Hahiroth. So at this early point in the journey the Israelites gained no ground towards Mt. Sinai as they did not advance. And as just discussed, an extra day was expended stopping the Amalekites.

Additionally, the Israelites did not do any travel on the Sabbath, so each Sabbath was a day where no distance was covered on their journey to the Holy Mountain, nor during their wandering during the subsequent forty years. The Sabbath was the holy day of rest. The biblical text makes this quite clear. In Exodus 16, when the Israelites arrived in the Wilderness of Sin they grumbled of being hungry. It was here that God provided manna to be gathered each morning. But on the day before the Sabbath,

God provided a double portion of manna because none would be available on the Sabbath. As the biblical text records, "Mark that the Lord has given you the Sabbath; therefore He gives you two days' food on the sixth day. Let everyone remain where he is: let no one leave his place on the seventh day. So the people remained inactive on the seventh day" (Exod 16:29–30). Every Sabbath the Israelites did not travel.

To summarize, the journey from Egypt to Mt. Sinai took forty-five days. The Israelites did not travel in a direct manner, requiring instead the need to travel from water source to water source and accounting for the need to find forage for the animals. They spent one day backtracking, so they journeyed no distance towards Mt. Sinai for at least this one day. They also did not travel on the day they had to deal with the Amalekites, so on this day too they did not make progress towards their goal. They did not travel on the Sabbath. There were six Sabbaths during the forty-five day it took to reach Mt. Sinai. While the Israelites took forty-five days to get from Egypt to Mt. Sinai, they only traveled for thirty-seven days. How far would they have traveled in thirty-seven days? The following chapter will elaborate on the distances traveled each day.

7

Sinai Peninsula

And they came to Elim where there were twelve springs of water and seventy
date palms, and they encamped there by the water.

—EXODUS 15:27

THROUGHOUT THIS BOOK, THE harshness of the desert, the lack of water,
the lack of pasturage, and the challenges facing anyone trying to survive in
this environment is described. This chapter further describes the logistics
issues faced by the Israelites as assessed in Table 1.

The peninsula today is a fascinating land with much to share and understand; it would have been even more so during the time of the Exodus.
It was as vast a desert then as it is today; dry, and rain falls rarely. But as is
the case with all deserts, this one too teemed with life where the presence
of water could be found. Insects, lizards, and snakes make the desert home
but a wide range of birds also have called Sinai home, including vultures,
several breeds of eagles, and both the eagle owl and the desert owl or tawny
desert owl, which used to be called Hume's owl.

Although hard to find today, in ancient times there were plenty of
mammals living among the rocks, brush, and dried wadi banks. Many ro-
dents that populate the planet's arid zones are also found here. Rabbits are
present as are the hyrax and the sand fox, the latter two very rarely seen
today, even by local Bedouin. There are larger species as well. Wild sheep,
goats, and ibex were present in greater numbers in the past but are now

rare due to centuries of predation by the Bedouin. These animals now tend to stay among the southern mountains or along the mountainous spine that runs along the length of the peninsula's western side. In the past the Sinai Peninsula boasted a broader range of larger animals that included lions, leopards, antelope, and even elephants. Today only the leopards are believed to remain and they are almost exclusively resident in the higher mountain slopes in the south.

The Sinai mountain range was formed more than six hundred million years ago as part of the Arabo-Nubian Massif. Over the ages, rains and melting snow created an interconnected maze of valleys and wadis that eventually filled the underground water catchment basins. The spine of mountains that runs along the peninsula's western side offered the best opportunities for water and grasses. The cluster of mountains at the bottom of the peninsula supported a wide range of life, including human life with numerous villages clustered among oases and wadis that are sprinkled around the valleys girding the mountains.

The mountain spine in the west can be a barrier to travel or to invading armies. Although not large, the mountains are sufficiently rugged and challenging for most travelers. There are two passes through these mountains and both are famous, especially to anyone familiar with Israel's wars with Egypt. These passes are Giddi Pass and Mitla Pass. Since 1948 both passes have required deliberate planning to counter their strategic value, both by the Egyptians and the Israelis. But the importance of these passes goes much further back in time.

Around 1170 the renowned Muslim leader Salah ad-Din, or Saladin, had a stronghold built on a small hill that commanded the eastern approaches into Giddi Pass. Saladin was the founder of the Ayyubid dynasty. His power base was in Egypt and he was a military strategist who deliberately planned defenses of Egypt from attack originating in the east. Giddi Pass is located along the second-most important east-west travel route through the Sinai and Saladin wanted to ensure this pass could not be used by an enemy. The stronghold never fell. It was finally destroyed during the 1973 Yom Kippur War. The Egyptians used the stronghold as a tactical observation post to support its ground forces that were pushing into the Sinai towards Israel. The Israel Defense Force air force bombed the stronghold and eliminated the Egyptian observers and destroyed the fortifications in the process.

During the Roman era the second largest city after Alexandria Egypt was located in the northwest corner of the Sinai Peninsula. Pelusium became a major port city and its location along the most important east west route through the Sinai ensured its prosperity for many centuries. The city was near both the Mediterranean and the eastern parts of the Nile Delta. The city was the site of many battles and conflicts. In 720 BCE Sennacherib, king of Assyria, failed to conquer the city. At the height of the Roman Empire, Pompey was assassinated in Pelusium after fleeing there for his safety. Pompey was one of the members of the First Triumvirate, which included Marcus Licinius Crassus and Julius Caesar. When he challenged Caesar for leadership of Rome, a civil war ensued. Pompey was defeated and fled, to no avail. In 1117 the city was razed by Baldwin I of Jerusalem, during the Crusades. It never recovered and today the site of the former city is mostly mudflats. There are three active archaeological excavations at the site and a number of finds uncovered reflect the glories of the ancient city. Many of the finds can be seen in Egypt's national museum in Cairo.

The Sinai Peninsula remains a place of fascination for many and treasures remain to be found. Because the Mediterranean coast of the Sinai was the main land bridge between Africa and the Near East, people and armies have been trekking across it for millennia. Indeed, when early humans migrated out of Africa into the Eurasian land mass, they crossed the Sinai Peninsula to do so. For these reasons many artifacts of antiquity, such as coins, clothing clasps, jewelry, and much more have been lost and await being found again. In 1972 a Bedouin man walking around five kilometers from the northwest town of Qantarra found a gold crown incrusted with jewels partially buried in the sand. He turned the crown over to authorities and it is now on display in the national museum in Cairo. It is surprising he surrendered this treasure. The Bedouin in the Sinai are not wealthy. The normal result of any ancient finds is for the finder to sell it, either up front in the market or on the black market. In this case, the crown is now a treasure for all to share and enjoy. It is displayed in the national museum and has been dated to the third century BCE.

In addition to the archaeological excavations near the site of Peleusium, less important ruins dot the Mediterranean coast. In the northeast corner, close to the Egypt-Israel border, is the town of El Arish. It is an old town that dates to antiquity. The same King Baldwin who razed Peleusium died in El Arish shortly after returning from Peleusium. El Arish is located eighty to ninety miles from Peleusium. During the Roman era, the legions traveled by foot throughout the empire upholding its security, the "Pax Romana." Rome's legions developed a policy as Rome rose to greatness, requiring a place of security wherever a legion stopped for the night to rest and sleep. In most cases this was a Roman city or town or a major fortification, many of which were spread throughout the conquered territories. But if a secure place was not available then the Romans built rectangular walled forts where one hundred soldiers, a legion, could overnight in security. The Sinai between El Arish and Pelesium held no cities or towns and the distance was too far for soldiers to march in a single day. The Roman legions were trained to march fifteen miles per day and then stop to rest. This is discussed elsewhere in this book. It took six days to march from El Arish to Peleusium. The Romans therefore built six forts at a day's-march distance between these occupied Roman communities. Today the shores of the Mediterranean have encroached on the land of the peninsula, in some areas up to two miles. Of the six forts only two remain; the others are presumed to have been submerged under the sea's waters.[8]

In 1981, following the last Arab-Israeli war, the United States took the lead to establish the Multinational Force and Observers (MFO) to help preserve the new peace between Israel and Egypt. The MFO was created after the United Nations was unable to set up a UN peacekeeping mission due to the threat of a USSR veto. Since its creation fully one third of the force of the MFO has been American soldiers. These soldiers were stationed in a camp created on the southern tip of the peninsula called Sharm el-Sheik. From the very beginning, the US soldiers took advantage of the opportunities to hike in the southern mountains and enjoy the water sports available from the off-shore waters that boasted and still boast one of the world's most beautiful coral environments. In 1987 several US soldiers spent a couple of days hiking and overnighting in the mountains. On their second night they decided to sleep inside a cave. In the back of the cave one of the men discovered the sword, shield, and chainmail of a Crusader knight. The soldiers surrendered the materials to the Egyptian authorities. These all ended up in the national museum and they are dated to roughly 1100 CE.

The weather in the Sinai swings through a wide range of conditions. It gets hot—over 100 degrees Fahrenheit—in the summer and the short winter can have days close to the freezing mark. These conditions were the same when Moses and the Israelites wandered in the desert. Rain rarely occurs but when it does it is often very heavy and intense. The rain may last only an hour or two, but an accumulation of two to four inches an hour is common. Heavy rains quickly fill wadis and flash flooding can destroy roads and lives. In 1988 Cairo experienced a once-in-a-hundred-year rain of several inches per hour for nine hours. Cairo is a desert city; it is not designed to drain away excess water and the city experienced flooding throughout. But the biggest problem was realized after the rains stopped. The rain washed many years of sand and dust accumulation off the buildings and into the streets. After the rain ended, the population found dozens and dozens of city streets cut off and blockaded by mounds of dust and sand that rose in heights to between six and fifteen feet. It took two days for the army and many civilian bulldozers, trucks, and bucket vehicles to remove these blockades. It was all quite unique.

One other weather phenomenon that plagued ancient peoples and people of today is sandstorms. They hit the Sinai as they affect any other desert environment. Sandstorms can be strong enough to block the sun's rays and can produce sustained winds for sometimes four to six hours that will literally blast the paint off cars and trucks.[9]

For all its harsh challenges, the Sinai has life, there is water, and over two dozen Bedouin tribes have made it home for centuries. One of the favorite adventures for hardy visitors to the southern Sinai and Gebel Musa, the currently accepted Mt. Sinai, is to climb the slopes of the mountain in time to witness the sunrise. The climb only takes a few hours and when the sun appears, dappling the many peaks surrounding Jebel Musa, the sight is truly one of the most beautiful in nature. Since the desert enjoys clear sunrises almost every day of the year, few visitors are disappointed.

The Sinai is a demanding and challenging environment. But it is also beautiful as any desert can be. And it is a fascinating place with an engaging and vital history. While never at center stage, the Sinai Peninsula has long been an important support actor in history.

8

How Far the People Traveled Each Day

Setting out from Elim, the whole Israelite community came to the wilderness
of Sin, which is between Elim and Sinai. On the fifteenth day of the second
month after their departure from the land of Egypt.

—EXODUS 16:1

"Up, DEPART FROM AMONG my people, you and the Israelites with you!
Go . . ." (Exod 12:31). With these words pharaoh told Moses to take the
Israelites and leave Egypt, capitulating to the will of God. The Bible says
that the Israelites journeyed from Rameses to Succoth, beginning their
journey to the Promised Land, which was to last forty years. They took with
them "very much livestock, both flocks and herds" (Exod 12:38), indicating
that the multitude that left Egypt included all the people, young and old,
able and infirm, and a very large number of animals. The number of people
and the animals with them would have had a major impact on how fast they
could travel each day of the journey.

Before considering how many miles this large group of people and
animals covered each day, it is important to also understand the challenges
and constraints they faced. The previous chapters considered some of the
physical challenges they faced and offered some idea of what the challenges
of traveling in the desert of Sinai would be.

This chapter addresses the assessment categories of distance and logistics in Table 1. At the beginning of this momentous journey, the Israelite

people were little more than a disorganized mass held together mostly by the will of Moses and their desire to be free. It was only after they reached the foot of Mt. Sinai that they became organized, and that was mostly due to the good advice Moses received from his father-in-law, Jethro. After the Israelites arrived in the Wilderness of Sinai and at the base of Mt. Sinai, and before Moses again communed with God, Jethro arrived with Zipporah and Moses' two sons. "Moses recounted to his father-in-law everything that the Lord had done to pharaoh and the Egyptians for Israel's sake, all the hardships that had befallen them on the way, and how the Lord had delivered them" (Exod 18:8).

The next day Jethro advised Moses on how to organize the tribes and from this advice Moses was able to put into place organization that allowed the Israelites to more efficiently travel, forage, and fight. They were able to manage each day more efficiently but they would still travel as they did upon leaving Egypt, similar to how a Bedouin tribe would travel either in the distant past or today. That Moses took his father-in-law's advice is not surprising and consistent with the culture of the time. Not only was Jethro Moses' father-in-law, he was also an older man with wisdom developed over many years that Moses would have valued. The Israelite culture of the time, as with many of the cultures in the Ancient Near East, granted significant respect to older people and particularly to successful older community leaders. And the latter was a good reason why Moses accepted Jethro's advice on organizing the former slaves. Jethro was a leader of an essentially successful Bedouin tribe. He spent all of his life among and leading people who made mobility and efficient movement a way of life. When he offered his suggestions to Moses, Jethro was imparting wisdom gleaned from many years of trial and error as well as learning from his own elders.

Bedouin tribes live in the Sinai today. As in the past they are mostly shepherds and herders. Then as now, they annually drive their animals from grazing lands in one season to other grazing lands in other seasons. These Bedouin traveled at the rate of their animals, which averaged approximately five to eight miles per day.[10] Today's Bedouin differ from their ancestors mostly in that today they have small pickup trucks and TVs. But these do not affect the distances they travel moving their animals; the rate of speed is determined by the animals. To relate this to other human travel in ancient times, the ancient Egyptian army traveled an average of seven to fifteen miles per day, depending on terrain, which was the trained marching distance of the Egyptian infantry.[11] The chariots could travel much faster, but for sustained travel the army speed was that of the foot infantry. When the Roman Empire rose to prominence, the Roman legions, among the best warriors or soldiers to have lived in the ancient world, were trained to march at a steady pace of fifteen miles per day, just like their Egyptian counterparts. They only diverted from this pace when military operations required them to force march, which was a pace averaging twenty miles a day, but this was the exception, not the rule. An army going into battle after being force-marched was already at a disadvantage against rested and ready foes.

The Israelites who left Egypt were not Egyptian or Roman warriors; they were former slaves without experience or skill in traveling distances on foot beyond moving animals between pastures. They were moving with animals and flocks as well as children, the frail, and the elderly. According to Exodus 12:38, the Israelites had "large droves of livestock, both flocks and herds." They would have needed to find sources of water and food along the route for these animals as well as for themselves, and they would have needed to allow time each day for the flocks and herds to graze and feed.

Nothing in the Bible says God gave the people and animals super abilities, so the conclusion can be made that they would have been slowed by the need to feed and water animals and humans, rest both animals and humans, sleep, and account for the unfamiliarity of the Israelites to sustained walking. The Bible says repeatedly that the freed slaves arrived at a location, sojourned, and then traveled to the next location. This means they halted and slept or rested before continuing their journey. They would have covered no more than six miles each day,[12] and very likely even less than that. The larger the group traveling, the slower its rate of travel would have been. The host of freed slaves would not have traveled in a straight line; they would have followed water locations and pasturage, further reducing the actual direct-line distance traveled each day.

One passage in the Bible seemingly says the Israelites traveled nonstop every day of the trip from Egypt to Mt. Sinai. Exodus 13:21–22 says, "And the Lord was going before them by day in a pillar of cloud to lead them on the way and by night in a pillar of fire, to give them light to go by day and by night." Elsewhere in the Bible it is clear that the Israelites sojourned or paused each day and often complained to Moses of being thirsty or hungry. The people and the animals were not especially endowed by God; they tired, thirsted, and needed to rest just as anyone would. They especially needed rest during the first weeks of their travels as their bodies adapted to the unfamiliar experiences of walking for sustained periods of time. This passage in Exodus says God provided a pillar of cloud to lead them during the day—remember that God was actually leading, not Moses. And at night there was a pillar of fire to protect the Israelites from the dangers that existed all around them. The last chapter discussed the fact that a larger variety of animals thrived in the Sinai Peninsula during the time of the Exodus. These animals included predators such as lions and leopards, and as the people slumbered the pillar of fire kept these threats at bay.

The biblical text shows a clear understanding of the hardships of travel with flocks and herds in the desert in ancient times. It is easy to think that flocks and herds represented sheep and goats, as these animals are usually represented in Bible stories and imagery. However, Numbers 7:87–88 notes that the Israelites also left Egypt with bulls and rams along with the expected sheep and goats. These larger animals were used in sacrifices at Mt. Sinai and their care and tending had to be taken into account along the journey.

Genesis 33:12–14 records the meeting between Jacob and his brother Esau. During this meeting Jacob gave gifts to his brother and Esau invited Jacob and his retinue to accompany him to Shechem. At first Esau invited Jacob to follow him but Jacob told Esau to travel home ahead of him. He told Esau that he could not travel as fast due to his animals and young children. "My lord (Esau) knows that the children are frail and that the flocks and herds, which are nursing, are a care to me; if they are driven hard a single day all the flocks will die. Let my lord go on ahead of his servant, while I travel slowly, at the pace of the cattle before me and at the pace of the children." Although these words are in Genesis, they show that biblical people understood how animals and children impacted travel times and distances, slowing any group to the pace of the slowest among them. Most of the animals were grazers, which would have further slowed the journey as they paused to capitalize on all edible growing things they encountered. When Jacob told Esau that the children were frail, he was not informing his brother that his children were all sickly and weak. Jacob was affirming the simple fact that small children, regardless of fitness level, do not have the stamina and endurance of adult men and women.

The Israelites were encumbered on their journey and these factors would have had an impact on the rate of march each day they traveled from Egypt to Mt. Sinai. This would have determined the total number of miles they would have traveled during the forty-five days it took them to reach Mt. Sinai from their departure from Goshen.

9

Numbers of Israelites in the Exodus

Then the Lord said to Moses, "When you take a census of the Israelites to number them, each man must pay the Lord a ransom for his life when he is counted. Then no plague will come upon them when they are numbered."

—EXODUS 30:11–12

ANOTHER OF THE MANY questions surrounding the Exodus and assessed in Table 1 above is the number of Israelites that left Egypt for the Promised Land. In this case, size mattered. The more people and animals that had to be moved, the slower the process would have been and the less distance this group of freed slaves would have traveled each day. The biblical text records that "600,000 men on foot, aside from children" (Exod 12:37) left Egypt. They brought with them "a mixed multitude and very much livestock, both flocks and herds." If there were 600,000 men on foot, the number of women, children, very old, and very young would have easily brought the total departing Egypt to close to two million souls.[13] These numbers have been problematic and for many decades a large number of books and articles have postulated that the host of Israelites was much smaller than 600,000 plus.

Numbers have always been a challenge of biblical hermeneutics for scholars. The simple task of finding water and food for this many humans and animals in as desolate environment as the Sinai Peninsula would have been almost impossible. In addition, during the period of the New Kingdom of Egypt, when the Exodus occurred, sometime between 1400 and

1200 BCE, the entire population of ancient Egypt was approximately two and a half to just under three million souls. The Israelites did not outnumber the Egyptians despite being prolific, according to the text of Exodus 1:8.

Population growth in Ancient Egypt[14]

The size of the Egyptian population at the time of the exodus is a challenge for scholars. Nothing to date has been uncovered to indicate that the Egyptian government maintained a census or, indeed, even showed interest in the size of its population. As for slaves in Egypt, nothing discovered indicates any list of slaves was maintained. This makes it very difficult to estimate the population of slaves or Egyptians during the Bronze Age or, indeed, at any time during Egypt's pharaonic period. It is nevertheless possible to accept that the population of Egypt was somewhere between 2.5 and 3 million souls around 1400–1200 BCE. This is due to the efforts of a number of scholars who have attempted to offer plausible arguments for population growth from the beginning of the pharaonic period, 3000 BCE, until the time of the Roman conquest of Egypt. Guillemette Andreu in his book *Egypt in the Age of the Pyramids* argues that the population was over two million by 1800 BCE. Karl Butzer is widely recognized as providing the most comprehensive scientific assessment of population growth in Egypt. In his book *Early Hydrologic Civilization*, Butzer identifies a very steady growth in Egyptian population from around 6000 BCE up to the Roman period. His analysis shows that the population was just under one million at the beginning of the Predynastic Period and rose to over five million when Egypt was finally conquered by the Romans around 30 BCE. Butzer extrapolates from the steady line of growth that the population was around 2.5–3 million at the time of the exodus.[15] As for the number of slaves, there is simply no date or evidence to definitively support a specific number at any given time period. Many scholars settle on the slave population of Egypt being no more than 10 percent at any time. This number is based for the most part on looking at the slave population of the Roman Empire, which never rose above 10 percent. There is also basis for this total of slaves on the cost of maintaining and supporting the population of slaves. So population numbers for Egypt at the time of the exodus will remain problematical unless and until some evidence is uncovered, probably by archaeology uncovering ancient evidence.

There has been widespread recognition among Bible scholars that numbers in the biblical text offer challenges to understanding. Understanding the numbers of exodus participants requires a concept of Israelite slavery at the time of the Exodus in the context of ancient norms. The Bible refers to slavery at several points that highlight the sources, status, duties, and treatment of slaves. The concept of slavery evolved over the centuries of Bible translations. Slavery was common in ancient cultures. Although it appears that most Israelite slaves were destitute at the time of the exodus, many were not; they were property owners with cattle, sheep, and other possessions that they either left behind or carried with them. Many Israelite slaves were assimilated into the social and cultural environment of Egypt prior to the exodus; in some cases, Israelite slaves were considered part of the Egyptian family unit, meaning that some may have not been prepared to leave. In Egypt, Israelite slaves built the grand treasure cities Pithom and Rameses, among other constructions. Still, because the Israelites continued to multiply despite their oppression, pharaoh worried that his Israelite slaves would rise up against Egypt.

And the numbers used for the total Israelites who departed Egypt are a good case in point. Dr. Kenneth A. Kitchen offered some good explanations in his book *On the Reliability of the Old Testament*. Some numbers in the biblical text present no problems for modern scholarship. They reflect the efforts of ancient scribes to be accurate in recording the events. Remember that accuracy was important; this book was intended to be an accurate historical record of the Israelite people and their relationship with God. The numbers "ten(s)" and "hundred(s)" do not give cause for confusion; they are not ambiguous and do not raise questions when they are used in the Bible.

As Dr. Kitchen noted, the only real question these numbers raise is whether they were accurately recopied down the centuries.[16] The challenges with the numbers in a case like that of the exodus started to emerge when "thousand(s)" came into use. Words describing numbers came into existence in history when there was a need for them. For example, according to the *Merriam-Webster Dictionary*, the first time the word "trillion" was recorded in use was in 1690. This was when human society found a need for this number. The same was true around the time of the exodus or a time prior with regard to "thousand." The term "thousand" was in use but very rarely, and the term used at the time had multiple uses. Like English, Hebrew has words that look the same but can have different meanings and these meanings are only apparent when the words are read in context. In Hebrew, the word *eleph* can mean "thousand," but not always. In Genesis 20:16 its meaning is clear, where the context reads ". . . a thousand pieces of silver." And in Numbers 3:50 *eleph* also means "thousand" in the context of ". . . the Israelites, 1,365 sanctuary shekels." But the word *eleph* is also used to refer to varieties of groups, such as a clan, a military squad, and a rota of priests and others. In the biblical text, *eleph* is used one way in Joshua 22:14 to refer to "*contingents* of Israel" and in Judges 6:15 it is used in another way: "Why, my *clan* is the humblest." The word used in these cases for "contingents" and "clan" is the same, *eleph*. Again, in 1 Samuel 10:19 *eleph* is used for the English word "clan": "by your tribes and *clans*."[17] In Hebrew, like often in English, context helps to determine the meaning of the word in question.

Hebrew vowels are often not expressed by full vowel letters, making for complicated word constructs. As Dr. Kitchen observed in his book, "So the question has been asked by many: Are not the 'six hundred three *thousand* five hundred fifty people' in such passages as Numbers 2:32 actually 603 families/squads/clans, or leaders with 550 members or squads commanded? Or some such analogous interpretation of the text?"[18] To clarify the point Kitchen made, another passage in the Bible, 1 Kings 20:30, can also serve as an example of this. Here the text records that a "wall fell on the 27,000 men." It is a stretch to accept that a wall fell and killed 27,000 men. However, if that wall fell on 27 officers, the fact is much more believable. In this case *eleph* refers to the squads these 27 officers commanded. The biblical text is accurate; what needs to be understood is the context, especially when words with more than one accepted usage are in play.

Did the Israelite host include 600,000 men on foot and associated women, children, elderly, and animals? In 1906 famed biblical archaeologist Flinders Petrie considered the two census lists in Numbers 1 and 26 in the context of the different meanings for the numbers. He concluded that the number depicting men under Reuben was not 46,500 men, but instead was 46 families of 100 people each. Thus, Petrie reasoned, the people in the Reuben tribe that migrated from Egypt to Sinai actually totaled about 5,500 men. Petrie was not able to account for the numbers of Levites and other figures in the Exodus, but he reasoned that the large numbers presented in the text of the Bible were probably the result of past rewritings that misrepresented what the original text recorded.[19]

After Petrie, other noted scholars have attempted to sort out the biblical numbering of the population of the Exodus. In 1958 George Mendenhall used Petrie's methodology and arrived at a figure of 20,000 Israelites departing Egypt. In 1987 Nahum Sarna took issue with Mendenhall, arguing that the figures Mendenhall used should have been used for clans, not just military squads. Another scholar, John Clark, in 1955 accepted the *elephs* in the biblical text to represent leaders. He then calculated the Israelite host that left Egypt totaled 140,000 souls. L. P. Wenham in 1967 also used the *elephs* for leaders but then concluded the Israelite total was closer to 72,000. In 1998 and 2000, John Humphries built on Petrie's insights and took a much more aggressive mathematical approach. He also recognized the different uses of the Hebrew *eleph* to identify totals of squads and what they consisted of. He determined that 596 squads would have totaled 5,730 men. Humphries's conclusion was that the total number of Israelites that left Egypt was between 20,000 and 22,000 people, which was close to the conclusion Mendenhall arrived at in 1958.[20]

It is impossible to determine how many people left Egypt for the Promised Land. A total numbering in the area of 20,000–40,000 would be realistic, based both on the population of Egypt during the time period of around 2,000,000 and the numbers of people the harsh desert environment of the Sinai Peninsula would have been able to support and sustain during the time period of 1400–1200 BCE.

The importance of the number of Israelites leaving Egypt, besides whether the environment of the Sinai could support them for 40 years, is in the daunting challenge Moses faced moving them from one Exodus itinerary location to the next. Even in the primitive time of the Exodus, the logistics of movement would have been very challenging. Every morning the people would have had to wake up and prepare their belongings for the day's journey. They would have had to be fed and whatever food they had had to be prepared or unpacked for consumption. During the time God provided manna, every day they would have had to collect and distribute it. The animals needed to be watered and fed, or allowed to forage if pasturage was available, which it often wasn't. The animals would have then been collected together under the supervision of herders and shepherds, children calmed and prepared for movement, and families gathered into their clans and the clans positioned into their places in the march line. All of this would have taken time, and the larger the body of people was, the longer this all would have taken. At the end of the day's journey, Moses would have needed to halt for overnight camp early enough so the last groups of travelers would arrive in the camp in time to get the animals cared for, the people fed and watered, and families off to sleep before too much of the night had passed. Once Moses' father-in-law, Jethro, helped him organize the Israelites according to appointed leaders, the distance traveled each day would have improved. But this happened once the Israelites arrived at Mt. Sinai. The going would have been much slower and more disorganized from the time they left Egypt until they arrived at the Holy Mountain, before they got organized.

Remember, it took 45 days to reach Mt. Sinai from Egypt, but only 37 days were actual travel days. The distance the Israelites covered each day averaged between five and seven miles. A simple multiplication of 45 days times seven miles would result in a total distance traveled of 315 miles. But they did not travel in a straight line and this does not take into account times they doubled back on the route or were delayed due to any number of reasons, such as the Amalekite attack or the crossing of the Sea of Reeds or days they did not travel at all due to the Sabbath. So, although the Israelites took 45 days to reach Mt. Sinai, they were only actually traveling along a nonlinear route for 37 days.

If they traveled every day in a direct route from Egypt to the Holy Mountain, one could multiply 37 by five and conclude the distance they traveled was 185 miles. However, again, the Israelites did not travel a direct route—far from it. Every day the Israelites would have traveled between five and seven miles, but, to use the euphemism "as the crow flies," the distance traveled to Mt. Sinai was more like three to five miles. Based on all these conditions, we can conclude the distance the Israelites traveled between Egypt and Mt. Sinai was between 75 and 120 miles at most. This distance corroborates Moses' request to pharaoh when these two leaders first met to take the slaves for "three days" to the Holy Mountain to sacrifice to their God. The three days may have been an understanding between Moses and pharaoh that the distance to the Holy Mountain was the distance pharaoh's chariots could travel in three days, or between 75 and 100 miles. This will be discussed in the next chapter. Further support for Mt. Sinai being close to Egypt's eastern borders will be offered in the next couple of chapters.

10

Moses Traveling Back and Forth between Mt. Sinai and Egypt

The Lord said to Moses in Midian, "Go back to Egypt, for all the men who
sought to kill you are dead." So Moses took his wife and sons,
mounted them on an ass, and went back to the land of Egypt;
and Moses took the rod of God with him.

—EXODUS 4:19–20

EVEN BEING GENEROUS, IT is hard to accept the freed slaves going much
more than a modest distance beyond the borders of Egypt. This chapter
addresses the distance traveled as assessed in Table 1. The site long accepted
as the location for Mt. Sinai in the southern Sinai mountains is, in relative
terms, a long distance from the borders of ancient Egypt. Key evidence that
biblical Mt. Sinai was closer to Egypt than previously postulated is offered
by the text of the book of Exodus, which records a number of trips made
by Moses to Egypt and back, by his brother Aaron to Mt. Sinai and back,
and by both of them to Egypt and back. All of these journeys occurred
before and during the time Moses traveled to Egypt to meet with pharaoh
to demand that pharaoh free the slaves.

For many familiar with the Old Testament, the events of the Exodus
began when Moses first encountered God on the Holy Mountain. Prior to
that, the events recorded in the book of Exodus, and in Genesis before it,

were preambles to what was to come. Moses had driven his father-in-law's flock to the vicinity of Mt. Sinai and decided to "look at the marvelous sight" (Exod 3:3) of a bush that was burning but was not consumed. As he approached, God told Moses to "remove your sandals from your feet, for the place on which you stand is holy ground" (Exod 3:5). This was how Moses knew the mountain was holy; because God told him. But it was only holy when God was there. Other than the events of the Exodus and God's interactions with Moses, Mt. Sinai had no other role in the history of the Israelite people. There is no text in the Bible indicating that the mountain was used for any holy or religious purposes before or after and there are no other documented records from antiquity that refer to Mt. Sinai.

In Exodus 3:1 the mountain is called "the mountain of God." This could have been an indication that the mountain was already considered a holy place, but due to the lack of any evidentiary text attesting to this, it is more likely that the term was more anticipatory and written into the biblical text by the author, Moses, or by a latter scribe.[21] God then told Moses he had chosen Moses to free his people from slavery in Egypt.

One of the sites marked in Figure 1 as proposed for Mt. Sinai is Har Karkom. It is largely rejected because the site is located within the boundaries of the land promised by God to Abraham. Esteemed archaeologist Emmaunel Anati favored Har Karkom in a beautiful book written about Har Karkom titled *The Mountain of God*. In this book Anati focused significant justification for his conclusions on the evidence he found at Har Karkom for burials and primitive religious sites. These justify the mountain being a holy place, according to Anati. However, the Bible does not say Mt. Sinai was a holy place. Had it been, Moses when he first approached the mountain would have prepared himself suitably for entering a holy place. But no, Moses had to be told by God that the ground he stood on was holy ground. Mt. Sinai was holy only when God was there. When the prophet Elijah fled there nothing is noted in the Bible that he had to be careful not to desecrate holy ground.

Getting back to the nearness of the mountain to Egypt proper, the passages of the Bible that are relevant to understanding the mountain's proximity to Egypt begin with Exodus 3:16. Starting here, the Bible records that God commanded Moses to "Go and assemble the elders of Israel." The elders of Israel were the leaders of the Israelite slaves and were slaves themselves. They were not free to travel any distance, so Moses had to go to them. Moses traveling from Mt. Sinai to meet with the elders was his first trip between the mountain and Egypt. After assembling them, God commanded Moses to "go with the elders to the king of Egypt" and ask that the Israelites be allowed to "go a distance of three days into the wilderness to sacrifice to the Lord our God" (Exod 3:18). This was not the time Moses was supposed to ask pharaoh to free the Israelite slaves.

Moses then met with pharaoh and asked that the Israelites be allowed to travel a distance of three days to sacrifice to God, nothing more. This is from Exodus 5:1–4 and is quoted at the beginning of chapter 1. The request for three days' distance could have been to test pharaoh or it may have been intended to deceive him; the Bible is unclear. It is also quite possible that the three days were an understanding between Moses and pharaoh that the Israelites would not go beyond the distance pharaoh's chariots could travel in three days, a distance both nobly raised Moses and pharaoh were familiar with and implicitly understood. Moses would not speak falsely to pharaoh, nor would God expect him to do so. Therefore, it is likely that Moses recognized that Mt. Sinai was a three-day journey by chariot from Egypt, something both pharaoh and Moses would relate to. After this meeting Moses returned to Mt. Sinai. This was the first round trip for him between the mountain and Egypt, but not the last.

In Exodus 4 Moses had returned from his first encounter with pharaoh. He now spoke with God and tried to convince God that he was unworthy of the task God was giving him. He asked that God give the task to someone else (Exod 4:13) and God got angry with him. God told Moses that he would have someone to speak for him and further told Moses, "There is your brother Aaron the Levite . . . *even now* he is setting out to meet you . . . he shall speak for you." (Exod 4:14–16, emphasis added).

Aaron was a slave and an older man. He was going to leave, or had already left, his home and servitude in Egypt to meet with his brother Moses at Mt. Sinai. He could not have gone for any length of time or he would have been missed and become a hunted runaway slave. Aaron was on foot; there is no biblical evidence that he traveled in any other way and as a slave it is unlikely he had access to any faster mode of travel. Since he was walking and aged, he could not travel great distances in the time he had. Aaron was going to meet with his brother and then return to Egypt before he was missed and a search for him was instituted. Furthermore, Aaron was not inured to traveling long distances by foot. As a slave, Aaron was used to labor that required him to use his arms, shoulders, and back. Slaves were not challenged to walk distances; this was not something they were accustomed to. Aaron had to be able to get to the mountain and return to his home in a short enough time as to not make his masters aware that he was gone. This is another point of evidence that Egypt could not have been far from the Holy Mountain.

Moses acceded to God's wishes that he become God's instrument to free the Israelite slaves. In Exodus 4:19 God told Moses that everyone in Egypt who sought his death since he fled Egypt after killing the Egyptian were themselves dead. On hearing this news, Moses asked his father-in-law's permission to go to his kinsmen in Egypt "to see how they are faring" (Exod 4:18). Jethro granted permission and Exodus 4:20 says that Moses traveled with his wife, sons (plural; there is now more than just Gershom), and pack animals to Egypt. They were en route to Egypt, having left the Holy Mountain. The Bible records during this trip "a night encampment" where a very odd encounter occurred between God and Moses, followed by an intersession by Zipporah, which ended the encounter (Exod 4:24–26).

All this occurred after God told Moses that Aaron was coming to visit him, but Aaron had not met up with Moses. Exodus 4:27 records that Aaron arrived at the mountain of God, where he met with Moses and kissed him. Understanding this text reveals that Moses and his family had gone to Egypt; they had met with his kinsmen and he now met Aaron at the Holy Mountain. By this account, Moses had made this second round trip to Egypt and back with his wife, sons, and animals and then met with Aaron, all while Aaron was traveling from Egypt to meet Moses and subsequently returning to Egypt. This records a lot happening between Egypt and Mt. Sinai and adds evidence of the distance between the Holy Mountain and Egypt.

Culturally, it would have been important for Moses to travel to Egypt to visit with his kinsmen. Family ties were strong among Israelites in Egypt, as they are for Jewish and Christian families today, and the customs and traditions then and now support this. Moses would have wanted his immediate family to be known among his kin, especially his mother and siblings. Since fleeing Egypt, Moses had not seen his mother or any of his other relatives. He now had a wife and two sons, whom he would have wanted his mother and relatives to meet and get to know. This trip would have been very important and necessary. The trip and visit were very consistent within the context of Israelite customs and traditions.

After meeting Aaron, Moses told him all that God wished of Moses. Moses and Aaron together returned to Egypt (Exod 4:29), where they assembled all the elders of the Israelites and Aaron shared with them all that

Moses had told him. This was yet another trip to Egypt after Moses settled his wife, sons, and animals back in their tents after returning from Egypt with his family.

In the beginning of chapter 5 of the book of Exodus, Moses and Aaron met with pharaoh and asked again that he allow all the Israelite slaves to travel three days into the wilderness to "sacrifice to the Lord our God" (Exod 5:3). At this point in the book of Exodus, Moses has still not asked pharaoh to free the slaves. Pharaoh's response was to deny the request and to increase the burden on the slaves, requiring them to maintain the quota of mud bricks without providing them with the necessary straw to make the bricks. In Exodus 5:22 Moses "returned to the Lord" and asked God why he was sent to Egypt, as he had only increased the suffering. That "Moses returned to the Lord" means he returned from his meeting with pharaoh back to Mt. Sinai to speak with God. This was Moses' third round trip between Egypt and the mountain. Moses specifically asked God, "why did you send me?" (Exod 5:22). He did not ask God, "Why am I here?," which he would have if he were talking to God from Egypt. He was not; Moses had returned to the mountain to speak with God.

Exodus 6:9 records "But when Moses told this to the Israelites, they would not listen to Moses, their spirits crushed by cruel bondage." Moses had once again returned to Egypt to meet with the Israelites to share with them what God had told him on the mountain. The slaves were already feeling the added burden imposed to them by pharaoh after Moses had asked that they be allowed to travel three days to sacrifice to God. Moses had returned to Sinai and spoken with God and he was now back in Egypt witnessing the suffering of the slaves resulting from maintaining the quota of mud bricks without being provided with straw to make the bricks. This was another instance of Moses "commuting" between Sinai and the capital of Egypt, where pharaoh was located.

Afterwards, Moses and Aaron again returned from Egypt to the Holy Mountain, Moses' fourth round trip. In Exodus 6:10–11 God met with Moses and commanded Moses to "go and tell pharaoh to let the Israelites depart from the land." This was the first time God instructed Moses to ask pharaoh to let the slaves go free. Moses replied, "The Israelites would not listen to me" (Exod 6:12). He said they "would not," not "will not," because some time—the time it took to travel—had passed and Moses was no longer located where the Israelites were; he was back at the mountain communing with God.

In Exodus 6:12 Moses again complained to God that the people would not listen to him because of his "impeded speech." In 6:13 God spoke to both Moses and Aaron,[22] giving them instructions regarding the Israelites and pharaoh. The text throughout Exodus 6 is very clear that God was speaking only to Moses. But in this verse God spoke to both Moses and Aaron, indicating that Aaron had again traveled to the mountain from his home and place of bondage to hear God's words.

In the next chapter of Exodus, chapter 7, Moses and Aaron had again returned to Egypt. They were now in the same location as pharaoh so they could communicate with pharaoh and do God's work to free the slaves and end the captivity. At this point in the biblical text, God spoke to Moses in Egypt, no longer at Mt. Sinai. The biblical text makes the distinction of noting when God was in Egypt and when he was meeting Moses at Sinai. Exodus 6:28 says, "For when the Lord spoke to Moses in the land of Egypt . . ." Here the Bible differentiates between Mt. Sinai and Egypt. God was speaking to Moses and Aaron at Mt. Sinai all through the earlier chapters of Exodus. Now, in chapter 7 the text of the book of Exodus has changed. Now when God was speaking to Moses it was "in the land of Egypt."

All of this affirms that Moses made numerous trips to Egypt and back and that Aaron also traveled between the two locations on several occasions. All of this would not have been possible had Mt. Sinai been further away from Egypt's eastern border, where Moses met pharaoh and pharaoh eventually agreed to free the Israelite people. In order for Moses to make his trips back and forth between Sinai and the meeting place with pharaoh, and for Aaron, his brother, to also make his trips, Mt. Sinai had to be located much closer to Egypt than has been considered to date. This is especially true in the case of Aaron because he was a slave and could not have been away for any length of time or he might have been recorded as a runaway slave.

So, Mt. Sinai could not possibly be in the Arabian Desert, or in southern Sinai, or even in the Negev region of present-day Israel; these locations are just too far from Egypt. All evidence points to a distance that two old men could safely and securely travel over and over again alone or together for three days in each direction.

11

Jebel Musa and Jebel Serbal

On the third new moon of the Israelites' going out of Egypt, on this day did
they come to the Wilderness of Sinai.

—EXODUS 19:1

TODAY MANY JUDEO-CHRISTIAN RELIGIOUS leaders, scholars, and lay people believe that Exodus 19:1 supports the position that Mt. Sinai is located
in the southern Sinai Peninsula mountains. Jebel Musa, Mt. Moses, has
long been the traditionally believed site of Mt. Sinai. This chapter addresses
two of the assessed criteria from Table 1: archaeology and scholars.

Today it is hard not to connect Jebel Musa with the Eastern Orthodox
monastery of St. Catherine.
Two mountains, Jebel Musa
and Jebel Catherine, stand
over the monastery, which
is one of the oldest, if not
the oldest, continuously occupied monasteries in the
world. Figure 6 is a contemporary view of the inside of
the monastery.

Jebel Musa rises to a
height of 2,285 meters, or

Figure 6: View inside the Monastery of St.
Catherine. Photo taken by the author in 1989.

50

7,497 feet. Jebel Catherine stands at 2,637 meters, or 8,651 feet, making Catherine one of the taller mountains in the Sinai Peninsula. There is no evidence, archaeological or otherwise, that Jebel Musa is the Mt. Sinai of the Bible. The claim that the mountain is one and the same dates back to the middle of the third century CE, when Christian monks began arriving in the area to find for themselves an ascetic life following the ideals of St. Anthony, who himself became a hermit in Egypt's Eastern Desert. Many of the Christians living in Egypt in the first and second centuries CE were fleeing Roman persecutions, which became severe during the rule of Emperor Decius Quintus Traianus, around 249–51 CE.[23] During this time, according to Dionysus of Alexandria, close to 144,000 Christians were killed in Egypt.[24] The Sinai became a favored area to flee to as there were no Romans deep in the peninsula and the conditions were what the ascetics were looking for.

The connection between Jebel Musa and Mt. Sinai first developed when these monks, or ascetic hermits, living in caves along the mountainsides, began to identify the mountain with the biblical Mt. Sinai. A small monastery was built that became a center of worship for the monks residing in the area. The claim that Jebel Musa was Mt. Sinai was given a boost by the area's association with the site of the burning bush, which is today located in the small "Shrine of the Bush" inside the monastery. The bush is considered by devout Christians a direct descendent of the burning bush from which God spoke to Moses.

In the early fourth century CE, Empress Helena, Emperor Constantine's mother, visited the monastery and ordered a chapel for the burning bush built. Today it is considered the holiest part of the monastery.[25] While she was visiting the area, Empress Helena also declared her view that Jebel Musa was the Mt. Sinai of the Bible. Empress Helena claimed to be a seer who possessed psychic powers and her declaration that Jebel Musa was the Mt. Sinai of the Bible carried a great deal of weight, such that the declaration remained an article of undisputed faith until modern times.

Joseph Hobbs wrote a book titled *Mount Sinai*. This title is one of the best (in this author's opinion) books written explaining the history behind Jebel Musa being Mt. Sinai. In his book Joseph Hobbs initially posited, based upon biblical text and the physical environment, that Jebel Musa is the biblical Mt. Sinai. He expanded upon his position by describing how religious and political leaders during the past sixteen centuries developed sites and reinforced beliefs using physical geographic features to identify where specific biblical events would have occurred. He described where others have cited Mt. Sinai, the cultures of the people who have lived in the region for the past several centuries, and the desecration of the mountain by visitors and construction near the mountain during the past fifty years.

Specifically, Hobbs cited his belief that the Bible provides the specific route and itinerary the Israelites would have used to reach and camp at Mt. Sinai. He referenced Exodus 12:37–41; 13:17–21; and 14:1–2[26]; Deuteronomy 1:6–19[27]; and Numbers 33:1–49.[28] He described the specific natural setting of Mt. Sinai by interpreting what the words found in Numbers 11:5, 31; 20:5; and Deuteronomy 8:7–8 mean as far as shapes of mountains and the movement of animals up to recent times.[29] However, he seemed to hesitate in his approach as he stated, "Scholars use varying assumptions about the date, the number of people traveling, the political situation, and the environmental context of the Sinai to argue for one of three possible routes of the Exodus."[30] He did not settle on one route.

Hobbs raised a key argument early in the book on the vagueness of any specific description of Mt. Sinai in the Bible even though historians throughout centuries have assigned meaning to biblical passages. Hobbs added to the uncertainty of where Mt. Sinai is located by noting, "Perhaps people are not meant to know where this mountain stands and be tempted to revere it rather than the message it stands for . . . It is a celestial place, which God placed off-limits to ordinary people."[31] As the biblical text records, "Take care not to go up the mountain or touch the edge of it. Anyone who touches the mountain will be put to death" (Exod 19:12). If this were the case, then his support that Jebel Musa is Mt. Sinai would be erroneous since the second half of his book described the growing number of people who live, visit, or manage facilities on Jebel Musa and support calling it Mt. Sinai, accomplishing the opposite of the biblical admonition.

Instead of being a powerful advocate for Gebel Musa being Mt. Sinai, Joseph Hobbs's book is much more a very well written and researched study of the Sinai Peninsula. In the book Hobbs described the physical environment of Sinai, as he calls it "a terrible and waste-howling wilderness." He also provided easy-to-read details about the Monastery of St. Catherine's, the Bedouin way of life, and especially the history of human involvement in the peninsula. For anyone wanting to gain a better understanding and appreciation of the Sinai Peninsula and its place in history, *Mount Sinai* by Joseph Hobbs is an excellent source.

Late in the fifth century, the Byzantine emperor Justinian I had a strong wall built around the monastery chapel and in 560 CE the Church of the Transfiguration was completed just before Justinian died. Dedicated to the Virgin Mary, the church became associated with St. Catherine of Alexandria and during the tenth century the Monastery of the Transfiguration became the Monastery of St. Catherine.

In the second and third centuries a number of mountains in the southern Sinai Peninsula served as home to the many Christians seeking the ascetic life of the time. Of these, Jebel Serbal gained many adherents for the title of Mt. Sinai. Jebel Serbal was an appealing contender for the location of God's Holy Mountain. The mountain is 6,791 feet tall, making Serbal the fifth tallest mountain in Egypt. The peak looms over Wadi Feiran, which is both well watered and fertile. Even today, Wadi Feiran supports a large Bedouin population thanks to the abundance of water in the area. In the late 1800s some scholars, such as Ludwig Schneller, concluded that Mt. Serbal was the best candidate for Mt. Sinai.

Schneller came to believe this based on his study of the exodus route, his analysis of how fast the Israelites would have traveled to reach Mt. Sinai, and his contention that the exodus itinerary location of Rephidim was located in Wadi Feiran.[32] A small monastery was built in the late second century but it and the claim that Serbal was Mt. Sinai were short-lived. Until recently, Jebel Serbal was a popular tourist site for many of the reasons it was considered the true Mt. Sinai in the past: a small convent is located in Wadi Aliyat, running along the base of the mountain, not far from Wadi Feiran. From its peak views of the Gulf of Suez and the mainland of Egypt across the gulf are often present. There are wells, small streams that never dry out, and oases, as well as ancient ruins and inscriptions also around the mountain and on its flanks. Looking at Mt. Serbal in Figure 7, it is easy to see how some could think this mountain was Mt. Sinai.

Once Roman emperor Justinian founded the monastery on Jebel Musa, the status of this mountain being Mt. Sinai was sealed for many Christians for centuries to come. The monks and hermits who

Figure 7: View of Mt. Serbal in the southern Sinai mountains. Photo courtesy of photographer Mike Luddeni.

were located at Mt. Serbal gradually relocated to Jebel Musa and the small monastery at Serbal was abandoned. Although there are few biblical reasons to consider Jebel Serbal as Mt. Sinai, some scholars, like John Lewis Burckhardt, decided one reason favoring Jebel Musa was more strategic than anything else: Jebel Musa was, and is, more defensible than Jebel Serbal or Wadi Feiran.[33]

The identification of the descendant of the burning bush being located inside the walls of St. Catherine Monastery was also an important argument for Jebel Musa being Mt. Sinai in the eyes of many Christians. The burning bush identification dates back to the earliest times of ascetics residing in the area. A monk named Ammonius chronicled the burning bush in a settlement of ascetics on Jebel Musa in the year 372 CE.[34]

Although the history of Jebel Musa, Jebel Catherine, and St. Catherine Monastery is rich and long, there is little based on the biblical text to validate Jebel Musa being Mt. Sinai. On the basis of travel time, Jebel Musa is too far for the Israelites to have reached it in forty-five days. It was also much too far for Moses to have traveled back and forth from the Holy Mountain to pharaoh the number of times he did, or for his brother Aaron, a slave, to have traveled away and back in a short enough time as to not be missed by his overseers.

When Moses asked pharaoh to allow the slaves to travel three days to offer sacrifices to their God, pharaoh understood this to mean the slaves would travel a distance his chariots could go in three days. The mountains of southern Sinai were too far for pharaoh's chariots to reach in three days even if pushed. Jebel Musa only started to be associated with biblical Mt. Sinai beginning around the fourth century CE.

Even the Jewish Roman historian Josephus failed to provide a location for the mountain in any of his many writings. As a Jew, he would have understood the value of knowing the location of Mt. Sinai and would have recorded it if he had known it. The fact that early Christian monks and aesthetics identified with Jebel Musa as Mt. Sinai is more likely due to their desire to have a holy place close to where they were living than to any biblical attribution.

In *Mount Sinai* Hobbs listed where other scholars believe that Mt. Sinai is located elsewhere and why.[35] In the end, however, Hobbs continued to focus on Jebel Musa based upon geographical and celestial, meteorological, and natural events. He did this again by describing how religious pilgrims and Christians fleeing persecution through the ages believed Jebel Musa and other locations were sought out as Mt. Sinai as a "logical and accessible place of retreat," but that these groups eventually tended toward Jebel Musa likely due to its remoteness and existing religious symbolism.[36]

Hobbs seemed to slip backwards from his insistence that Jebel Musa is the real Mt. Sinai as, in *Mount Sinai*'s chapter 4, he described the Monastery of St. Catherine's reason for existence and its role in reinforcing this site as Mt. Sinai since 565 CE. His further description in his book's chapter 5 about how the mountain has been shaped physically and metaphorically by Christian and Muslim visitors during the centuries (but particularly during the Israeli occupation in the 1970s) provides further credence that Jebel Musa may not be the mountain in fact, but has been identified as Mt. Sinai because visitors so much want it to be.

It would be inappropriate to discount Jebel Musa as the site of Mt. Sinai due to the sheer length of time and the faith supporting it as the Holy Mountain enduring for so long. Based on the biblical text, however, it is not the true Mt. Sinai.

12

Rameses: City or Region

The length of time that the Israelites lived in Egypt was four hundred and
thirty years. At the end of the four hundred and thirty years, to the very day,
all the ranks of the Lord departed from the land of Egypt.

—EXODUS 12:40–41

EXODUS 12:40–41 OFFERS TO us the opportunity to define from where the
exodus started. There is compelling justification for Mt. Sinai being much
closer to Egypt that comes directly from the biblical text. This chapter corroborates the assessment of distance supported by the Bible in Table 1.

Mt. Sinai should be searched for in the western area of the Sinai Peninsula, not far from the Gulf of Suez. The Holy Mountain would not be far
from the Bitter Lakes and the area of the northeastern Nile Delta, which
would be consistent with Moses' request to pharaoh that the people be allowed to travel "Three days into the wilderness to sacrifice to the Lord our
God" (Exod 3:18). As discussed earlier, Moses asked pharaoh to allow the
Israelites to travel not at the pace of the old or the young or the flocks,
which was how they actually traveled during the exodus, but rather at the
pace of pharaoh's chariots, which could travel up to twenty-five miles a
day, or thirty miles when pressed.[37] It would not have mattered to pharaoh
how far or how fast a population that included old people and babies could
travel in a day. Moses would not have wanted to give pharaoh any clues that
he intended to leave Egypt permanently with all the slaves and their flocks.

Exodus 12:37 says the Israelites "journeyed from Rameses to Succoth." This was the beginning of the departure; most of the slaves would have been living in the Nile Delta area and primarily in the eastern parts of the delta. Rameses was a well-known area in the eastern delta that predated the exodus and would have served as a convenient frame of reference for future generations. Furthermore, Joseph and his family first settled in Egypt in the region known as Goshen, which was located within the larger region of Rameses. Consistent with the manner that cities and important places are recorded in the Bible, Rameses was regarded as an important location, so it is listed first whenever noted in the Bible. Moses honored the region that had accepted Joseph by declaring it as the departure site in his text of Exodus. In the spirit of the biblical narratives, the Israelites made a full circle, arriving and settling in Rameses and then departing from that same area after the sojourn.

There is one other reason to explain why Rameses was accorded the honorary recognition of being the place of departure for the Israelites. The region of Rameses was where the remains of the patriarch Joseph were interred waiting the time when these remains would be removed from Egypt and carried to the Promised Land. Joseph was one of the sons of Jacob. Jacob had been blessed by God and renamed Israel, not to be called Jacob again (Gen 35:10). Later in Genesis, after Joseph became the Egyptian vizier and second to pharaoh, Israel set out from Canaan to see his son Joseph before he died. During that journey Israel was called by God and told, "fear not to go down to Egypt, for I will make you there into a great nation. I Myself will go down with you to Egypt, and I Myself will also bring you back; and Joseph's hand will close your eyes" (Gen 46:3–4). In this text from Genesis, God reaffirmed his covenant with the Israelites and his promise to bring them to the land of Israel, the Promised Land.

Shortly before Israel died, he exacted a promise from Joseph that Joseph was to have him buried in Canaan. Joseph promised to do this, fulfilling God's promise to Israel that he would go to Egypt and when he died Joseph would have him buried in his homeland of Canaan. All of this gave the Israelites a clear understanding that Joseph was the inheritor of his father's legacy. To the Israelite people who had settled in Egypt, Joseph became the symbol of Israel to them. When Joseph was about to die, he made the "sons of Israel" (Gen 50:25) swear to take his bones to the Promised Land when "God noticed them" and they departed from Egypt to that Promised Land. The sons of Israel were all the descendants of the sons of Israel (Jacob).

Later in Exodus, when pharaoh freed the Israelite slaves, Moses had the bones of Joseph carried along so that he would be buried in the Promised Land according to his wishes (Exod 13:19). Joseph's bones had rested in the region of Rameses and when the Israelites departed from Egypt Joseph's remains went with them. In a very real sense, "Israel" departed Egypt from Rameses as God promised and the biblical text recorded.

13

Jethro and Midian

Then Moses bade his father-in-law farewell, and he [Jethro]
went his way to his own land [Midian].

—EXODUS 18:27

THIS CHAPTER HIGHLIGHTS HOW the biblical text and distance from Egypt
are assessed in Table 1 to determine the location of Mt. Sinai. Exodus 18:27
explains that when Jethro was with Moses at Mt. Sinai he was not in the
land of Midiam, and when he left Moses he was returning to his home in
that land. Jethro, Moses' father-in-law, is a pivotal character in the recount-
ing of the Exodus and the significance of the location of Mt. Sinai. He was a
Midianite high priest, a very important personage in Midian society.

Chapter 3 of Exodus begins with Moses tending the flocks of his
father-in-law and driving them into the wilderness and coming upon
"Horeb, the mountain of God" (Exod 3:1). Horeb has long been recognized
as another name for Mt. Sinai. Nothing in the biblical text states that Horeb
was in Midian. Indeed, the Bible does not state that the priest, the daughters, the shepherds, or Moses were in a land called Midian when Moses
first encountered Jethro's daughters after fleeing Egypt. Many scholars have
overlooked this point and the movie *The Ten Commandments* seems to
have perpetuated this conclusion that they are in proximity of Sinai.

Moses fled from Egypt after killing an overseer. The Bible does not say
how long he traveled from Egypt before he encountered the daughters of the

priest of Midian. The Bible is silent on this and where the land of Midian was. Popular belief, such as reflected in the movie *The Ten Commandments*, by Cecil B. DeMille, says that Moses traveled forty days from the time he fled Egypt and encountered the daughters of Jethro, but the Bible does not substantiate this. As for the forty days cited in the movie, it is possible that someone advising DeMille on the exodus story referred to the Hebrew Midrash *Sefer haYashar* (Book of the Corrected Record), which suggested that Moses wandered forty days until arriving near the camp of Jethro.

The length of Moses' wanderings is not important for this book. Forty is one of the numbers considered significant as a long, approximate period of time that separates two distinct events or characteristics in both the Old and New Testaments. Moses wandered for forty days. Jesus spent forty days in the desert. Forty is important in other places in both testaments of the Bible.

The Bible only records that Moses helped the daughters of Jethro and later chose to marry the eldest daughter and become part of Jethro's family. The next biblical text talks about Moses and his family, now including a young son, herding flocks in the vicinity of the Holy Mountain.

Numbers in the Bible are often symbolic and serve as other cases of biblical hermeneutics that challenge scholars. Numbers represent an important cultural point being made by the biblical writer(s). Three days' travel time from Egypt to Mt. Sinai may have been the distance pharaoh's chariots traveled, but the number three also had important religious or cultural significance.

As to where Midian was and its relationship to Mt. Sinai, it was common practice among ancient nomadic people to identify themselves by their land name wherever they were. Midian was certainly a place and the Midianites themselves identified the place as their home location during the Bronze Age. Midian was also the identity of a Bedouin people who traveled with their flocks from the Arabian Desert to the Mediterranean coast of Canaan. This is common practice by the Bedouin in the present day as well.[38] Moses could have encountered the Midianites anywhere along their migration route and the Midianites would have referred to where they were as Midian. But they would only do this when they moved as a tribe. Individuals or individual families traveling through the Sinai Peninsula would not refer to the land where they were during their travels as Midian. As we will see shortly, this was clearly the case when Jethro traveled to Mt. Sinai to meet Moses, when he and the Israelite host arrived there.

A land called Midian has been recorded on maps dating from "Roman times onward"[39] but nothing earlier, at least nothing so far discovered. In chapters 22 and 31 of Numbers as well as chapters 6–8 of Judges, the Midianites were found in regions of Moab and as far west as the Jordan River. In an article published in *Vetus Testamentum* in 1975 titled, "Midian: A Land or a League," by William Dumbrell, the Midianites were identified as a "large Late Bronze Age League"[40] that exercised power over the entire area that later was controlled by the Nabataeans. This area included all of the Sinai Peninsula.[41]

Moses could have easily encountered his future wife and father-in-law anywhere within this large area and they would have identified where they were as the land of Midian. It is unlikely that Moses traveled to the land depicted as Midian on Roman maps after fleeing Egypt. To do so would have meant crossing the Gulf of Aqaba or passing through the Arabah, both daunting enough that his passage and the challenges of making a crossing of either would have been recorded in the Bible. Additionally, the time it would have taken to make either of these crossings would have been much greater than that allowed for in the time it took the Israelites to travel from Egypt to Mt. Sinai.

Even if Moses went on to the land of Midian located in the Arabian Desert, much time passed between his first encounter with Jethro and Moses leading his father-in-law's flocks to the base of Horeb. After Moses was welcomed into the Midianite family, the Bible says Moses was driving the family flock in the wilderness and came to Horeb. This all happened after his marriage and the birth of his son. Much time had passed, probably much more than just a few years, and Moses likely would have made the trek from east to west and west to east many times while moving his father-in-law's flocks. And again, there is no clear evidence in the Bible for where Horeb was. It could have been anywhere along the migration route of the Midianites, between the Mediterranean coast of Canaan and the western regions of the Arabian Desert.

However, there is an inscription dating from the fourteenth century BCE that refers to an area just outside Egyptian lands where the nomads worshipped Yahwe. This Egyptian inscription says this mountain was located "just outside Egyptian lands as the 'land of nomads who worship Yahwe."[42] This is another indication that Horeb, or Mt. Sinai, was located closer to Egypt than has been traditionally assumed.

The point to note about where Midian was is to understand ancient Bedouin culture. The Midianites would have referred to wherever they were during their annual migrations as the land of Midian. They were pastoralists and according to the biblical book of Judges the Israelite leader Gideon drove the Midianites into western Palestine, close to the Mediterranean coast (Judg 7:17–24). According to the book of Genesis, the Midianites were descended from Midian, the son of Abraham, and his second wife, Keturah, meaning Midian in this case was located in southeastern Canaan.

Genesis 37:28 records that Midianite traders pulled Joseph out of the pit his brothers had cast him into. The traders then sold Joseph to the Ishmaelites, who in turn brought him to Egypt, where he was again sold. At the time, Joseph's family all lived in Canaan, so it was quite common for Midianites to annually be found along the eastern Mediterranean coast. At the time of Joseph, Midianite traders were clearly active in Canaan.

One can conclude that the tribe of Midianites would call wherever they and their flocks were Midian. These lands at that time were not the possessions of specific kingdoms or empires. Where the Midianites wandered was the western Arabian Desert, the Sinai Peninsula, southwestern Jordan, and Canaan. Of these lands, only parts of Canaan were possessed by minor kingdoms, leaving much of the land to be used by whoever wished to. None of these lands came to be identified with the Midianites until early in the Roman period.

There is another relevant passage in the Bible that helps to clarify that Mt. Sinai was not in the land of Midian but along the migration route of the Midian traders and shepherds. Once Moses and the Israelites reached Mt. Sinai, Jethro traveled to meet him, bringing with him Moses' wife and two sons, Gershom and Eliezer. Exodus 18:1 records that Jethro "heard all that God had done for Moses and for Israel."

Jethro was the priest of the Midianites. He would have been both a powerful and influential leader of the Midianite people and nation. This text in the Bible makes it clear that his influence and authority gave Jethro the wherewithal to have people keep him informed of what was going on in Egypt and what was transpiring to, and because of, his son-in-law, Moses. Jethro was probably at his permanent home in the eastern land of Midian, located in the Arabian Desert, during the travels of the Israelites to Mt. Sinai.

When he learned that Moses and the Israelites were getting near Mt. Sinai, Jethro sent a messenger to tell Moses that he was traveling from his home location to Mt. Sinai. The biblical text records the message Jethro sent to Moses: "I, your father-in-law Jethro, am coming to you, with your wife and her two son" (Exod 18:6). Jethro delivered Zipporah and her sons to Moses in the wilderness, "where he (Moses) was encamped at the mountain of God" (Exod 18:5). Then, in Exodus 18:27, "Moses bade his father-in-law farewell, and he (Jethro) went his way to his own land."

After meeting with Moses, and after providing Moses with good counsel to better manage the large body of people now relying on Moses, Jethro left the Wilderness of Sinai to return to Midian. He came to Moses with Moses' small family and probably whatever retinue of servants and family he was accustomed to have traveling with him. However, he was not traveling at the head of a large Midianite group, or the tribe, as he was when he first met Moses, when Moses protected his daughters at the well. At that time the Midianites traveling with Jethro were sufficiently large enough that they called wherever they were "the land of Midian."

Now, Jethro left the same land around Mt. Sinai, or Horeb, but the Midianites were not with him, so he did not acknowledge it as Midian; rather, he left this land to return "to his own land." The mountain was closer to Egypt and not in proximity to where the priest of Midian maintained his permanent residence.

14

Routes Out of Egypt

And it happened when pharaoh sent the people off that God did not lead
them by way of the land of the Philistines though it was close, for God
thought, "Lest the people regret when they see battle and go back to Egypt."
—EXODUS 13:17

IN ADDITION TO DISAGREEMENTS among scholars about where Mt. Sinai
was located, there are also questions regarding the route the Israelites took
when they left Egypt en route to Mt. Sinai. Exodus 13:17 offers a clue to
where the Israelites did not go. This chapter looks at the common routes
through the Sinai Peninsula, why they are, and which route the Israelites
most likely took to reach Mt. Sinai. At the same time, we recognize that
since the time of Moses the desert terrain and environment has changed
dramatically. So, this chapter provides background for the Table 1 assessment categories of biblical text, archaeology support, and distance.

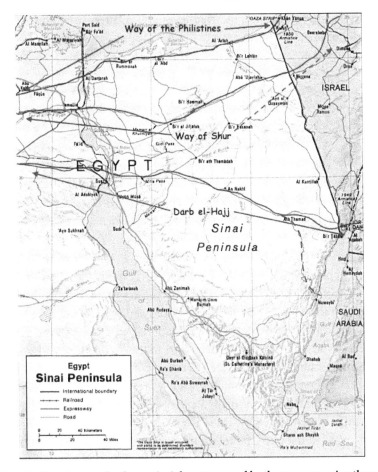

Figure 8: Map showing the three principle routes noted by three arrows going through the Sinai Peninsula from east to west. Additionally, the primary southern route is also depicted as a red line running down the western side of the peninsula

Figure 8 shows the three principle east-west routes ancient people used to travel from Egypt into Canaan and lands beyond Canaan. The named lines originating from Heliopolis in Egypt depict these routes.

The Sinai Peninsula was never a destination itself in ancient times. It was important, and in some time periods vital, because it was the principle land bridge between Africa and the rest of the Eurasian land mass. When Egypt became a great power, Sinai was the route the Egyptian armies took to expand their empire north and east.

When Egypt's enemies sought to conquer Egypt, the Sinai was again the route they took to get to Egypt. As Egypt was first being established, the people who lived along the Nile River and its delta were blessed with centuries of unencumbered time to build and secure their empire because the vast western desert of Egypt and the Sinai to the east, before the Way of Horus was established, were significant physical barriers that few nearby kingdoms were equipped to overcome. By the time such kingdoms grew sufficiently powerful to breach these obstacles, Egypt was powerful enough to overcome them.

When Egypt was dominant in the region, the Egyptians found sources of copper, malachite, turquoise, and salt in the Sinai and for a time mined these. Minor routes from Egypt to these mines were established. Some still exist as paved roads but most have disappeared into the sands. All of the routes through the Sinai Peninsula developed over many years, in some cases hundreds or even thousands of years.

As humankind spread out of Africa into the Ancient Near East and beyond, nomads and travelers sought ways through the desert. Those that ventured forth either discovered water sources to sustain them or died. The locations of water and pasturage were shared and slowly, over time, routes became known. None were direct or straight routes. They followed the water sources and eventually carried travelers to the destinations they sought. Because the water is so scarce, there were not many routes. The routes of the past became the roads of today. There are few roads in the Sinai Peninsula and especially in the interior roads are sparse. Anyone traveling in the Sinai will quickly understand why. There is little to attract visitors or commerce and today, as in the past, the roads are mainly used to get from one place beyond the Sinai's borders to another place beyond its borders.

In ancient Egypt travel routes generally followed eastern Nile Delta waterways through Goshen and ended in Memphis. The land between the Nile River and the Bitter Lakes and Lake Timsah was called "wilderness" in ancient times, for good reason. This land was desolate and water was almost impossible to find, so most routes were located outside this land.

Today a number of canals have been established running from the Nile up to the Bitter Lakes. These canals have allowed the Egyptians to turn part of the wilderness into farmland. However, even today there is not much beyond these canals and it is almost impossible to find roads. In ancient times, one route that did go south of the Bitter Lakes took travelers to where the port of Suez is today on the northern tip of the Gulf of Suez.

Finding any villages or settlements in this wilderness today is rare and those that can be found are close to the Bitter Lakes or the Nile River, or along the canals that did not exist at the time of the exodus. The reason is the same as it was in ancient times: lack of water. This was a lesser trade route but it was used. Although Figure 8 shows the three main routes into and out of Egypt, it was not as simple as that. These are the major routes; there were a few lesser routes as well.

Moses, as a former prince of Egypt, would have been familiar with all the major travel routes through the eastern deserts. Each represented a possible threat of invasion that he would have been required to be familiar with. He also would have known many if not all the lesser routes. When Moses fled from Egypt, he almost certainly took one of the three east-west routes until he was out of Egyptian territory. We can speculate that at that point he may have used a lesser route until he encountered the Midianites and the daughters of Jethro.

The three main routes through the Sinai were all east-west routes. They are depicted in Figure 8 as dark lines. Today these routes are paved and remain three of the principle highways through the peninsula. The northernmost route was a coastal road along the Mediterranean that went from present-day Qantara to Gaza. This route generally followed the contours of the ancient Way of Horus, or the Way of the Philistines. This was the most regular route in ancient times connecting Egypt to Canaan and considered the most threatening route that enemy armies could use to attack Egypt.

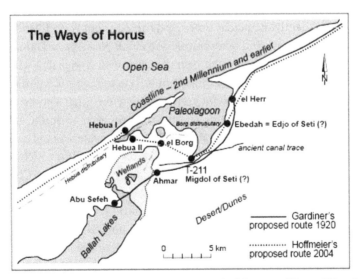

Figure 9: Map of northern Sinai at the Egyptian end of the Way of Horus (Way of the Philistines) showing fortifications against threats from the east.
Courtesy of Dr. James K. Hoffmeier.

Egypt's defensive bulwark of forts and towers were built on its northeastern border primarily to defend against enemy armies approaching along this route.[43] Figure 9 offers a good depiction of the fortifications built to protect Egypt from threats coming from Canaan. These fortifications and the fact that this was the major route into Egypt from the East have been referred to earlier as reasons why God took the people away from this path, as he did not want the freed slaves encountering concentrations of Egyptians for fear of conflict.

Another northern route used to travel to and from Egypt was the "Way of Shur" (see Figure 8). This route went from present-day Ismaelia across the Sinai to the south of the Way of the Philistines to the present-day Israeli city of Beersheba. Although this route was more inland, it passed a number of low mountain ranges, all of which have oases and wells today and had fresh water sources in the ancient past.[44] Genesis 16:7 references a water source along this route when an angel of God found Hagar by a "spring of water in the wilderness, the spring on the road to Shur." The presence of water made this route possible for travelers going to and from Egypt.

The third route in the northern part of the Sinai was called the Darb el-Hajj. This name was given this route when Muslim pilgrims made it a regular land route from Egypt to Mecca. The route passed the town of Suez on the northern tip of the Gulf of Suez and went into the Arabian Desert via Taba and the modern Israeli city of Eilat. It is not known if this route was used frequently in ancient times. Today it does not go to Eilat; instead the route bends south and takes travelers to either Neweiba or Dahab, both small villages on the coast of the Gulf of Aqaba with ferries that will carry vehicle and foot traffic from the Sinai Peninsula to the coast of Saudi Arabia.

There was a less important route through the Sinai Peninsula that went south. In ancient time this was the only route to go south. It is depicted in Figure 8 in red. The main reason for this route was the existence of the Egyptian copper mines located at Serabit el-Khadim, which will be discussed later in the book. During the Roman times when early Christian pilgrims were subject to persecuted, this route became important for those fleeing the persecution. It ran along the western Sinai coast, past Serabit el-Khadim and the town of Abu Rudeis, and into the mountains of the southern Sinai. This route led to Jebel Musa as well as Jebel Serbal and Jebel Catherine, all located in the southern Sinai mountains. However, before the second and third centuries when pilgrims were using this route, it was unimportant beyond Serabit el-Khadim.

Because the Sinai Peninsula was never a primary destination itself, the three important travel routes were east to west as travelers were going to Egypt or Canaan or places beyond these. Traveling south through the interior of the Sinai was fraught with challenges, especially the challenge of fresh water. The best north-south route was along the western coast, where it paralleled the mountain chain running down the western side of the peninsula and then into the southern mountains. The southern mountains boasted many sources of water, including oases with year-around water, streams and wadis that were water filled much if not most of the year, and wells. It was very possible that water and sources of food, including plentiful game, as well as solitude, offered ancient Christian pilgrims the attraction of settling among the mountainsides of places like Jebel Musa, Jebel Catherine, and Jebel Serbal. They were well beyond the reach or interest of any powerful nations. These then became holy places and their appeal rose exponentially.

Traveling through the Sinai Peninsula has never been an easy thing. Anyone spending any amount of time traveling around the Sinai Peninsula will observe this with graphic clarity. The land is harsh and unforgiving.

Figure 10: View of a desolate southwest Sinai not far from Abu Rudeis.
Photo taken by the author in 1989.

Besides the scarcity of water, fierce sandstorms can last hours and halt all movement. The scene in Figure 10 is very typical of the open desert of the Sinai central region. In ancient times, such as during the Exodus, water was at a premium and people always traveled from a known source of water to another known source of water. As a result, travel routes were never direct but always winding and twisting. The challenges of travel were compounded when people traveled with animals, as the Bedouin do today and the Israelites did during the Exodus. As a result, there were several minor routes that evolved over time in the Sinai desert.

Two of these routes were digressions from the Darb el-Hajj route and both brought travelers to the area of Kadesh Barnea in modern western Israel. One route near the middle of the peninsula at the town of el-Nakhl veered northeast until the traveler arrived around Kadesh Barnea. The other route diverted sooner out of Egypt, going northeast just past Mitla Pass and traveling through Bi'r Hassanah, then veering almost due east until arriving at Kadesh Barnea. All of these travel routes were secondary for ancient people or armies, but they were used enough to be of note. The harshness of the land and the scarcity of water and pasturage very much determined where and when routes could be made useful to the nomadic Bedouin in the past. Figure 11 shows a broad view of the landscape not far from the central Sinai town of El-Nahkl. This is very typical of the interior of the peninsula. It is clear that the environment was and is dry and harsh.

Figure 11: View of the terrain of central Sinai looking east and not far from the town of el-Nakhl. Photo taken by the author in 1989.

There were two routes that generally took travelers from today's Eilat, at the tip of the Gulf of Aqaba. Both developed in the Common Era and went north; one to Gaza or Beersheba and the other to the Dead Sea. The route to Gaza was an important trade route as it passed by or through communities that developed on the northern tip of the Gulf of Aqaba. This route would have offered a fairly direct way of getting from Mecca and Medina to Gaza and even to Jerusalem, and vice versa. These routes touched or went through the Promised Land and thus do not factor into the route the Israelites followed during the Exodus. Although they are mentioned here, these routes were not entirely in the Sinai Peninsula or they just skirted the edges of the peninsula.

There were other routes going through the Sinai Peninsula but they were all mostly variants on the main three routes described above. One thing was common about all the routes. There were known water sources along them. Otherwise the Bedouin would have never known them or used them. The main routes were in central or northern Sinai, where they supported activities associated with international commerce or military operations. The routes in southern Sinai did not serve military purposes and only modestly supported trade until late in the Bronze Age and into the Iron Age. Instead, the southern Sinai routes were developed for the exploitation of the few natural resources to be found in the peninsula. Among these were copper, manganese, and turquoise.

The exception in the south was the route along the coast that allowed pilgrims and theological ascetics to reach the mountains, especially Jebel Musa after Justinian had the monastery built there. As will be discussed, the likely route of the Exodus generally followed the known travel route along the western side of the Sinai Peninsula. This route differed mostly in that it traveled along the eastern edge of the wilderness between the Nile River and the Bitter Lakes until it crossed the Yam Suph between the Bitter Lakes and then continued south along the eastern side of the southern Bitter Lake.

The next chapter will discuss the route the Israelites took out of Egypt. It is a variation of the southern route discussed above. Instead of terminating at Serabit el-Khadim, the Israelites turned east to reach the Holy Mountain before reaching this location.

15

Departure from Egypt

And Moses said to the people, "Remember this day on which you went out of Egypt, from the house of slaves, for by strength of hand the Lord brought you out from here, and unleavened stuff shall not be eaten."

—EXODUS 13:3

IN THE BOOK OF Exodus, the ten plagues ended with the deaths of the first-born Egyptians. Recorded in Exodus 12:29, following the deaths pharaoh finally freed the slaves and Moses and the people took their first steps towards the Promised Land. Moses knew where Mt. Sinai was located; he had been back and forth from the mountain a number of times as discussed earlier. But God proceeded to lead the people away from Egypt. The route they took was not the way Moses used to travel back and forth from Egypt. This chapter uses assessment of the Bible and scholarly texts in accordance with Table 1 to narrow the location of Mt. Sinai.

As Exodus 13:17 notes, "God did not lead them (the Israelites) by way of the land of the Philistines, although it was nearer." God told Moses that he was concerned the Israelites would have to fight the Philistines. He was also concerned the Israelites would encounter large concentrations of Egyptians and Egyptian military border defenses. These too God wished his people to avoid. His concern was that they did not have the heart for a battle so soon after leaving Egypt and would turn back to Egypt and slavery, which is all they had known for many generations.

Instead God led the people via a roundabout route taking them through the wilderness and across the Sea of Reeds. The crossing of the Sea of Reeds, or the Yam Suph, will be discussed in the next chapter. The land of the Philistines was in Canaan, along the Mediterranean coast. In Exodus 13:17 God said this way was closer to Mt. Sinai but more dangerous. Traveling to the land of the Philistines would have been along or parallel to the Way of Horus, well to the north. This route would have brought the freed slaves to Mt. Sinai quicker, which is an admission that the northern route was closer to Sinai than other routes to the mountain. This is another instance of the Bible affirming the proximity of Mt. Sinai to Egypt.

The Bible says the journey began at Rameses in the delta (Exod 12:37). Rameses has been discussed earlier. Most likely the Israelites departed from the land of Rameses rather than the store city of Rameses. This book has already discussed the rationale for this. From Rameses the Israelites journeyed to Succoth. The Bible is also not clear where Sukkoth was located and therefore it is not evident how far that first period of travel was for the Israelites. Archaeological excavations at Tell el-Maskhuta in Wadi Tumilat have uncovered an ancient site that may be the site of Sukkoth or it may be the site of Pithom, though it could well be someplace else entirely. If Tell el-Maskhuta was Succoth, it was approximately thirty miles from Rameses, which would have been a strenuous journey for the Israelites, who were not accustomed to marching long distances.

The Bible does not say how long it took to travel from Rameses to Succoth but it probably took a total of three days, based on how long it took for the Israelites to reach the Sea of Reeds. The route is consistent with the biblical text describing that God led the Israelites in a roundabout way to the wilderness at the Sea of Reeds. The accepted site of Sukkoth is close to the northern end of the Bitter Lakes and the Sea of Reeds, the Yam Suph.

Succoth is referred to in a number of places throughout the Hebrew Bible. It was the location where Jacob settled and built a house after he parted from Esau in Genesis 33:17. This is also the text explaining where the name Succoth came from. Jacob built booths for his cattle and called the place Succoth after the booths. In the book of Exodus there is scant reference to Succoth and nothing to indicate where it was located. It is unclear where Succoth was located. It is recorded as being in the Jordan Valley in 1 Kings 7:46, in Egypt in Genesis 33:17, and again in the Jordan Valley in Psalms 60:6.

In Judges 8:4–9 there is a paragraph about Gideon chasing after the kings of Midian, Zebah, and Zalmunah. In this text Gideon asked the people of Succoth for bread for his soldiers. In reading the text, some scholars have concluded that Succoth must have been located in the Jordan River valley.[45] Succoth could not have been in the Jordan River valley because it would have been impossible for the host of freed Israelites to travel to Succoth from Rameses in a single day, or even three days as it says in the Bible they did. Yet the confusion persists as in 1 Kings 7:46 again the text seems to clearly place Succoth somewhere in the Jordan River valley. There are other biblical texts that conflict with the Exodus texts about where Succoth was located.

What is most likely is that there was more than one Succoth, one in Egypt close to the wilderness where Etham was located, and another in the valley of the Jordan River. This is speculation, but one source has recorded that there may be a connection between Succoth and *Tkw*, an area located to the west of modern Ismaelia.[46] It is not unprecedented for two or more different locations to have the same name and it is possible that this is the case here, but the Bible does not offer any clues to support this, so there is only scholarly conjecture.

Exodus 12:37 only notes that the Israelites journeyed from Rameses to Succoth. Exodus 13:20 says, "They (the Israelites) set out from Succoth, and encamped at Etham." Etham was a place at the edge of the wilderness. From Sukkoth the Bible says the people next traveled to Etham (Exod 13:20), where they encamped. Succoth was about a day's march from the wilderness, which was most likely the wilderness between the Nile River and the Bitter Lakes since the Israelites were still in Egyptian territory at this time. So Etham was located at the "edge of the wilderness" (Exod 13:20).

From Rameses and other locations, God led the Israelites away from the area of the eastern delta. Not only did this route distance the people from possible contact with the Philistines, it also led them away from potential confrontations with the Egyptians. The route led into the wilderness. We know this because the Bible says so. Egypt's population was centered on communities built up along the Nile River and the tributaries within its delta. Geographically, this made sense then as now.

Egypt was a desert land and not far beyond the waters of the Nile River it was almost impossible for large groups of humans to settle and live. Both a lack of water and a lack of arable land of necessity made the shores of the Nile the only places for humans to settle, with rare exceptions.

In ancient times the land between the Bitter Lakes and the Nile River was a wilderness where almost nobody lived. Even today this area is sparsely populated. It was a safe land for the Israelites as long as they could find water and grazing, and they had God to guide them.

The Nile Delta was well populated and the eastern delta was at risk of predation from threats moving west from Canaan. For that reason, the Egyptians created a powerful defense barrier along the eastern border that consisted of natural bodies of water like Lake Timsah, as well as canals, and both walls and a string of fortresses. While all of this was designed to keep enemies out of Egypt, it was also a potential danger for the newly freed slaves, so God led the Israelites away from these regions. In doing so, God led the people away from the well-traveled Way of Horus and the Way of the Philistines. This led away from the forts, fortifications, and developments around Lake Timsah, Lake Ballah, and the canals connecting them to the Mediterranean. (These are depicted in Figure 9 in chapter 14.)

Avoiding these regions is also a reason Lake Ballah and Lake Timsah are not good candidates for the Sea of Reeds. They were too close to fortifications and defenses well populated by the Egyptians, and avoided possible contacts with the Philistines located beyond the defenses on Egypt's eastern border. The Israelites were familiar with these areas and the text of the Bible indicates they were unfamiliar with the crossing site at the Sea of Reeds, thus the "sea" at the crossing location was unnamed. This will be discussed further later on.

The Bible says the Israelites encamped at Etham. The actual location of Etham is not yet known, but it was most likely located in the wilderness well east of the Nile but still west of the Bitter Lakes. Why the Israelites camped at Etham is not stated in the Bible but there were two very good reasons for them to do so. One reason would have been to rest both the people and the flocks that went with them. Their journey was just beginning, but because these people were without experiences or endurance for lengthy walking, the first few days would have been the most difficult as they inured themselves to the unfamiliar exertions. These people had been slaves for generations. They were used to hard labor, but it was labor that required back, shoulder, and arm strength. They had no experiences with extended walking, which uses completely different muscles. Simply put, after a few days of travel these people would have needed to rest, especially the very young and the elderly. A second reason for stopping at Etham would have been to allow Israelites from more distant communities to travel and join the main body under Moses. It would have taken time and the encampment of the main body would have given other groups time to reach Etham.

After the encampment at Etham, God told Moses to turn back and camp at Pi-Hahiroth, which was near Migdol and Baal-zephon. The Bible offers no explanation as to why God wanted the Israelites to essentially backtrack the way they came. Additionally, like Etham, it was not clear where any of these three locations were. *Migdol* was a Semitic term for "tower" or "watchtower" and also an Egyptian word for "fort," "fortification," or "stronghold" around the time of the New Kingdom, which would have been the same time as the Exodus.[47] There is a relief of Pharaoh Seti I at Karnak that shows the pharaoh returning from a campaign in Canaan. The images show the Egyptian forts that were located along the Way of Horus and identify the third fort by the name Migdol.[48]

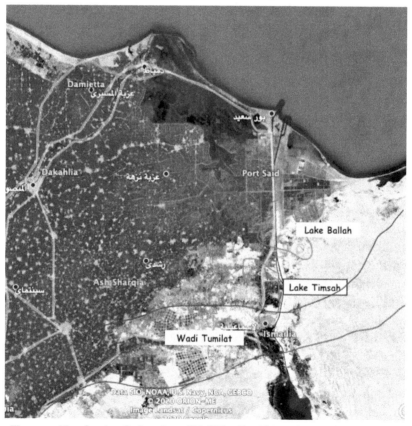

Figure 12: Map showing the location of Wadi Tumilat. This wadi, one of the largest in the Sinai Peninsula, extends well west of where Lake Ballah and Lake Timsah were in ancient times.

The conclusion from this is that the Migdol of the Seti I relief is possibly the same Migdol as the location in Exodus 14:2. Although the two settings where Migdol has been identified cannot be definitively connected, it is nevertheless reasonable to accept that the Migdol of the Bible was almost certainly located in the eastern delta near the Sinai desert not far from Wadi Tumilat. This supposition is based on recognizing that God's instructions to backtrack were not intended to place the Israelites in any greater risk from Egyptians. Figure 12 is a map locating Wadi Tumilat. While the backtrack is not explained, it is probable the reason was based on the availability of water. The backtrack was not back to Etham, but to Pi-Hahiroth, which may have been for a source of water that the Israelites needed then.

The third location listed in the Bible that God directed Moses to bring the Israelites to was Baal-zephon. Baal was a Canaanite deity and Baal-zephon most likely refers to a site where this Canaanite deity was worshiped in Egypt. There are several locations in the eastern delta where this deity was worshiped, any one of which could be Baal-zephon.[49] Like Etham, it is probable that the Israelites stopped at Baal-zephon because water and food for the animals could be obtained there. Worshippers of Baal would not be favorable or closely aligned with Egyptian authorities and could have been sympathetic to these people fleeing the Egyptians. The Bible also records that the place God directed the Israelites was near the sea and the Israelites were instructed to encamp facing the sea. The Bible here does not at first provide the name of the sea the Israelites were to face, but a few lines later[50] the Bible identifies the sea as the Sea of Reeds, *Yam Suph*, discussed in detail in the upcoming chapter, titled "The Sea of Reeds."

It is at this location that one of God's most singular miracles in the entire Bible occurred; that of parting the sea to allow the Israelites to escape the chariots and warriors of peninsula. Pi-Hahiroth was a community, possibly one with an influential Canaanite presence, located not far from the water connection, or isthmus, connecting the two Bitter Lakes. It was here "by the sea, near Pi-Hahiroth, before Baal-Zephon" (Exod 14:9), where the Israelites were encamped. They paused to allow Israelite slaves from other parts of Egypt to catch up with this main body. This also allowed pharaoh and his pursuing army to also catch up with them. Pharaoh believed he had the former slaves trapped between his army and the sea. This sea was only referred to as the Sea of Reeds, which is an identification, not a proper name. With no clear description in the Bible, including in Exodus 14:10–31, it is reasonable to conclude that this sea was unfamiliar to the Israelites.

The fact that the sea was unfamiliar is important. Scholars have in the past concluded that the miracle of the crossing had to occur near either Lake Ballah or Lake Timsah. But both of these lakes would have been familiar to the Israelites; they were both located in the eastern delta near settled areas and in close proximity to the Egyptian border defenses and forts. During the Egyptian New Kingdom, these lakes were connected by canals and in turn connected to the Mediterranean. The remains of ancient ports have been archaeologically uncovered in both lakes. Had the crossing occurred at either location, the name of that lake would have been recorded in the biblical text.

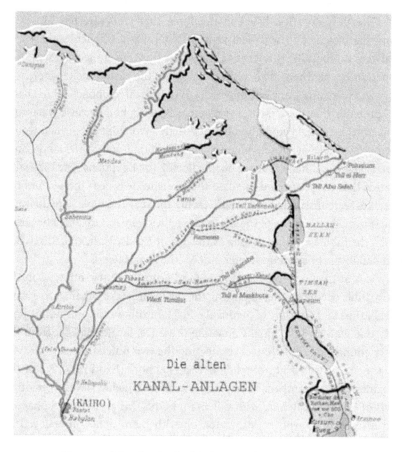

Figure 13: Map showing both Lake Timsah and Lake Ballah,
referred to on the maps as seas. Courtesy of Dr. Gary Byers.

The Bitter Lakes were at the eastern end of the wilderness separating the Nile from the lakes. This wilderness was an inhospitable region with a sprinkling of tiny communities and, most tellingly, these lakes had no recorded names as they were unimportant and infrequently visited. These lakes were located far from areas where the Israelites would have settled or where the Egyptians, requiring the presence of slaves, would have developed any projects. When Moses fled from Egypt he probably would have taken a more familiar route into the Sinai before meeting his future father-in-law, Jethro. He possibly traveled past the area of present-day Ismaelia, just north of the Bitter Lakes. But whatever path Moses took did not matter; God, not Moses, led the Israelites to Mt. Sinai. The Bitter Lakes were larger in ancient times than either Lake Ballah or Lake Timsah and could have easily been mistaken as a sea.[51]

On early post-Roman maps, both Lake Timsah and Lake Ballah were often shown as seas, much as Lake Tiberias in northern modern-day Israel is also called the Sea of Galilee. Figure 13 is a good example of this. The map is a German production and both Lake Ballah and Lake Timsah are identified as seas; "See" is the German word for "sea."

Other candidates for the sea crossing and for the Sea of Reeds will be discussed later. However, the Red Sea was much too large and deep to be the Sea of Reeds, including the Gulf of Suez on its northern tip. The Gulf of Aqaba, which has been offered as the Sea of Reeds, was too far distant from Egypt to be consistent with the biblical text and will also be discussed later in this book.

The parting of the water by God followed by the escape of the Israelites and the destruction of pharaoh and his army is an integral part of the Passover story that is retold every spring on the anniversary of the event according to the Bible. The Bible records God's instructions to Moses that his chosen people remember the Passover "throughout the ages" (Exod 12:14). After the events at the Sea of Reeds, Moses led the people into the Wilderness of Shur.

Although Figure 14 shows the Wilderness of Shur encompassing virtually the entire north of the Sinai Peninsula, the biblical text says that Shur was the wilderness east of the isthmus of Suez and was probably named for a defensive wall built by the Egyptians to prevent entry to Egypt from the east. Using this theory, the biblical Wilderness of Shur actually refers to the Wilderness of Etham, which is located just east of the isthmus in Figure 14.

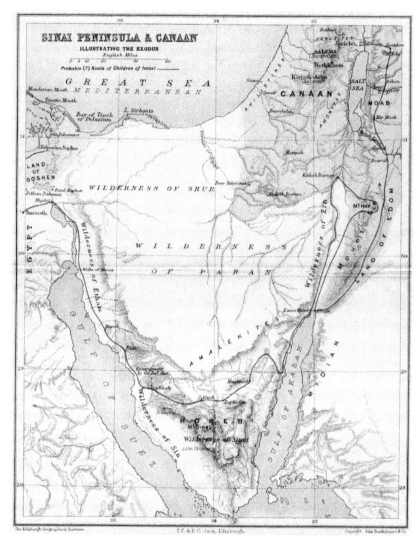

Figure 14: Map showing one location for the wildwrness of Shur.
From ancientexodus.com, used by permission of Dr. Glen Fritz.

The Bible says the Israelites traveled three days in this wilderness until they came to Marah. That means if they departed the Sea of Reeds between the Greater and Lesser Bitter Lakes and they traveled between five and seven miles per day as discussed earlier in this book, Marah was located approximately where the "r" is in "Wilderness of Etham" label in Figure 14.

At Marah the people complained of being thirsty for lack of water. After admonishing them, God had Moses throw a piece of wood into the bitter water at Marah, which sweetened it and allowed the people and animals to quench their thirst. A case can be made for Marah's location. Not far from where Marah's location is marked on the map is Uyun Musa, today called the Wells of Moses or the Fount of Moses. Today this location has an abundance of sweet water. There are a number of oases with brackish water in them, but there are also plenty of sweet well water sites in this location.[52] Thus, the Israelites could have found the brackish water first and then the sweet water with God's guidance.

God then led the people to Elim, where they found twelve springs of water and seventy palm trees and they were commanded to encamp beside the water (Exod 15:27). The only water that matches the text of the Bible is the Gulf of Suez. Elim was within sight of the gulf where the Israelites encamped. The Bible does not say how long they encamped but they probably stopped here to refresh themselves and their livestock and spent one night in camp before moving on.

There is no archaeological or extant evidence identifying the location of Elim. However, the Bible offers a very clear description of the surroundings that offers scholars clear evidence of Elim's location, as opposed to the lack of evidence for other locations along the route. This is an excellent example of examining the geography to help understand the truth on the ground the Bible is explaining. The Bible says that at Elim there were both plentiful palm trees and a dozen springs; Elim was almost certainly located in Wadi Gharandel (see Figure 15 below), which is reputed to be the best-watered site in the western Sinai.[53]

This area is located approximately nine miles south of the Well of Moses. The Well of Moses is not far from the town of Suez on the northern tip of the Red Sea, as seen also in Figure 15. All of this makes Elim a very important location for determining where the Israelites traveled en route to Mt. Sinai. The biblical description of Elim as a place with plentiful palm trees and a dozen springs offers a key geographical description along the route to Mt. Sinai. There is no other place in western Sinai that matches this description offered by the Bible for Elim. Indeed, there is no other site in the entirety of the Sinai Peninsula that matches this description. Elim had to be located in Wadi Gharandel not far from the Gulf of Suez. It is also a supportable location for where the host of freed slaves would have found themselves after thirty days of traveling.

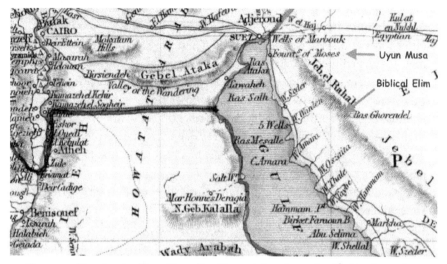

Figure 15: Map showing Uyun Musa, Ras Gharendel, and a mark added by this author for the location of Elim. Extract from map researched and copied at the United States National Archives and Records Administration on May 20, 2016.

The Bible says that after they left Elim the entire community arrived at the Wilderness of Sin. At this point, the biblical text recorded that the community came to the wilderness on the "fifteenth day of the second month after their departure from the land of Egypt" (Exod 16:1). This means that thirty days had passed since the Israelites were freed from pharaoh's dominion. The definitive comparisons between Elim and the wells and trees located at Wadi Gharandel, along with the time it would have taken the Israelites to arrive at Elim after crossing the Sea of Reeds between the Bitter Lakes, offers compelling support for this route of the exodus from Egypt to Mt. Sinai.

From this point until the Israelites arrived at Mt. Sinai, the route was, at best, unclear and the names of places identified in the Bible have not been found, or there are different locations contending for the right to be declared *the* biblical place. According to Numbers 33, the Israelites encamped in the Wilderness of Sin, meaning they spent the night resting themselves and their animals, and then traveled to Dophkah (Num 33:12) and encamped. Following the encampment, they traveled to Alush (Num 33:13) and again encamped. From Alush the Israelites traveled to Rephidim and remained overnight. Then, according to the text of the Bible, the people set out from Rephidim and next they encamped in the Wilderness of Sinai (Num 33:15). At this point the destination of Mt. Sinai, the Holy Mountain, had been reached.

Where the Bible records the Israelites encamping, it was only for one night in each case. God had a pillar of fire protecting the Israelites during the night hours and a pillar of cloud leading them during the day. They hurriedly left Egypt so they did not carry any excess of belongings with them. They did not set up elaborate abodes when they stopped and could easily have decamped each morning to get moving as quickly as possible.

Chapter 3 already described the number of days it took to travel from Egypt to Mt. Sinai. Another way to determine how long it took the Israelites to reach Mt. Sinai is to consider the biblical text recording it took thirty days to reach the Wilderness of Sin. From Sin, fifteen days can be added for the time the Israelites traveled from the wilderness to Dophkah, from Dophkah to Alush, and from Alush to Rephidim and finally to the Wilderness of Sinai. Rephidim was the last stop before the Israelites arrived in the Wilderness of Sinai. The biblical text says the Israelites encamped at each of these places and then they traveled on. This book contends that each encampment was for only one night and the total time it took to reach the Wilderness of Sinai from the Wilderness of Sin is offered as fifteen days.

One additional event occurred at Rephidim and before the arrival at Sinai. This was when Amalek "came and fought with Israel" (Exod 17:8). The Amalekites were marauding nomads who attacked the vanguard of the marching Israelites. This was a "surprise attack" (Deut 25:18), which resulted in an additional day being added to the duration of travel from Egypt to Sinai. Therefore, from two different perspectives it is reasonable to conclude that the duration of the journey from Egypt to the Wilderness of Sinai and the foot of the Holy Mountain, Mt. Sinai, was a total of forty-five days. The Israelites did not travel nonstop for forty-five days. The actual travel time to their destination was thirty-seven days.

There are questions regarding how long the Israelites stopped before crossing the Sea of Reeds, whether for more than a night, as Moses awaited God's guidance on how they would circumvent this obstacle, or just one night. When pharaoh arrived and God parted the waters, the Israelites crossed and their journey continued.

From the Wilderness of Sin the Israelites turned east towards Mt. Sinai.[54] They traveled eastward for twelve days until they arrived at the Wilderness of Sinai and Mt. Sinai itself. In twelve days the Israelites would have traveled approximately forty to fifty miles.

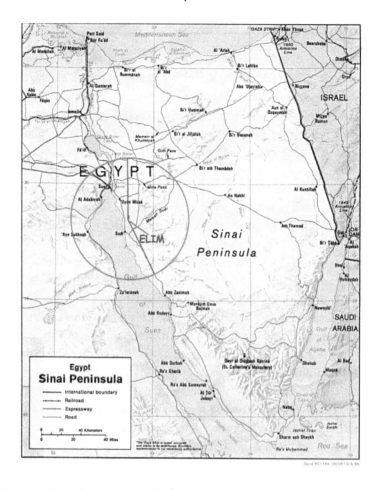

Figure 16: Circle shows the author's learned assessment of the approximate distance traveled by Israelites from Elim to the Wilderness of Mt. Sinai. Map provided by the author from the period when he was a member of the Multinational Force and Observers, MFO, a civilian peacekeeping force in the Sinai Peninsula.

Today's Middle East Bedouin, particularly tribes in the Sinai Peninsula, offer some insights into how long it would have taken for a migrating family group to wake up and organize before starting out. On average, Bedouin tribal groups traveling from one pasturage to another averaged between five to seven miles a day and usually not more than five. One of the reasons they only travel five to seven miles per day is that it take one to two hours to wake up and prepare to move, they can only travel one mile per hour with their animals, and they need to stop one to two hours before bedding down so they can reset their tents and prepare their evening meal. Today, modern Bedouin enjoy the benefits of owning small pickup trucks; they can start their animals moving before they have broken camp and set up their next camp before their herds arrive at the next campsite—so today, despite the trucks, the movement continues to be based more on traditional campsites, where in the past where they needed to break down and set up camps before/after flocks moved.

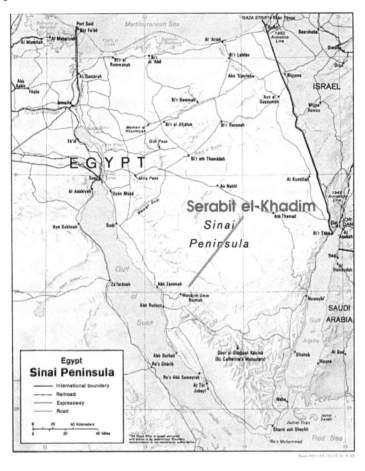

Figure 17: Location of Serabit el-Khadim in the Sinai Peninsula. Location added by the author.

Based on the evidence and the point where the Israelites turned east and traveled to the Wilderness of Sinai, Figure 16 shows a radius within which Mt. Sinai should be sought (with the area located to the right, or east, of the blue lines shown).

The Israelites turning east when they did is also evidence of Mt. Sinai being located in this part of the Sinai rather than further south. Had the Israelites continued down the western spine of the peninsula, they would have encountered the Egyptians again. Just to the east and a bit north from present-day Abu Rudeis are the ancient Egyptian copper mines of Serabit el-Khadim.

Serabit el-Khadim, Figure 17, was an ancient Egyptian mining camp where copper and turquoise were mined. In addition to the mines and living areas for the miners and guards, there was also a temple to Hathor located at the site to satisfy the religious requirements of the Egyptians working and living here. Serabit el-Khadim was located several kilometers inland from the present-day coastal town of Abu Rudeis. The ruins are still present (see Figure 18 below). Although there was only a minor military presence at the mines, the passing of the large host of Israelites would have been noticed and the Israelites would have become aware of the mining camp, which then would have been recorded in the Bible as a historical note. That Serabit el-Khadim is absent from the biblical text is reasonable evidence that the Israelites did not come within detecting distance of the site en route to Mt. Sinai.

Figure 18: Serabit el-Khadim as it looked in 1989 when this photo was taken by the author. The Bedouin in the picture was the author's guide to the site and behind him is the entrance to the temple of Hathor.

16

The Sea of Reeds

And Moses stretched out his hand over the sea, and the Lord led the sea with
a mighty east wind all night, and He made the sea a dry ground, and the
waters were split apart. And the Israelites came into the sea on dry land, the
waters a wall to them on their right and on their left.

—EXOD 14:21–23

THE SEA OF REEDS is very important to the Exodus narrative. Exodus
14:21–23 points to it as the Lord's miraculous avenue of departure. The
location of the sea is not identified in the Bible and there is no extant evidence of its existence or location. The location of the sea is a geographical
necessity in assessing, through Table 1, the location of Mt. Sinai because of
the importance of the crossing. Locating the Sea of Reeds through assessment of the Bible and scholarly text, geography, distance, and logistics con-
tributes to the overall effort of locating the Holy Mountain. The Israelites
traveled some days from their departure point to this sea, where several
miracles occurred. Among these were the parting of the sea by God for the
Israelites to pass, and the subsequent drowning of the Egyptian army and
pharaoh, who had given chase to destroy the escaping Israelite people after
pharaoh had a change of heart about freeing the slaves.

Today many Bible readers and believers still refer to this famous site
as the Red Sea, which has been the biblical translation of the ancient Hebrew text for centuries. However, in the last hundred years critical study

and analysis of ancient biblical texts and translations, including the Dead Sea scrolls found at Qumran, have brought to light evidence that the old translation of "Red Sea" is incorrect. Increasingly scholars and laypeople are coming to accept the Hebrew text סוּף-יָם, *yam suph*, not to mean "Red Sea" but "Reed Sea" or "Sea of Reeds" instead. The word *yam* means "sea" and *suph* is the word for "reeds" or "rushes." As with some other words in the Bible, the Hebrew text סוּף-יָם can have multiple meanings and can also represent "Sea of the End" or "distant sea."[55] Indeed, because the Sea of Reeds was located well inside the eastern wilderness of Egypt, the translation "distant sea" may be what Moses was actually stating. We simply cannot know for certain since *yam suph* has several equally valid translations.

Before describing the Sea of Reeds, there is a biblical text that offers an important clue to the location of this sea with regard to where the Israelites departure point was, or at least where Moses departed from pharaoh's presence.

Chapter 10 of the Exodus story talks about the eighth plague, that of locusts. Locusts were one of the worst natural disasters to occur in North Africa, then and now. When God visited the swarm of locusts upon Egypt, it would have brought terror and fear among the Egyptians, probably more so than any other plague but the tenth, the death of the first-born. The Bible says the locust invasion on that occasion was the worst ever experienced, never to be matched again (Exod 10:14). According to the text, pharaoh "hurriedly" called for Moses and Aaron and asked them to have this "death" removed. Moses, believing pharaoh was finally going to set the Israelites free, appealed to God to remove the locust scourge. Here, in the biblical text, God responded, He "caused a shift to a very strong west wind, which lifted the locusts and hurled them into the Sea of Reeds [*yam suph*] . . ." (Exod 10:19).

The locusts were not swept away to oblivion, nor did they just disappear. The Bible is specific: God made them all drown in the Sea of Reeds. The text says a strong west wind caused this to happen.

The strong west wind carried the locusts away from where pharaoh and the Egyptian population were suffering from this plague. The locusts were swept west across the empty desert wilderness between the Nile and the Bitter Lakes. Geographically, the Bitter lakes were in the right location to have been the sea the locusts were blown into. Just north of the Bitter Lakes, Lake Ballah and Lake Timsah were more directly west than either of the lakes from where Moses and pharaoh were when God cast the locusts into the *yam suph*. However, for the same reason neither of these lakes were the Sea of Reeds, neither of them could have been the sea the locusts were blown into. The Bible only says *yam suph*; had the locusts been hurled into either Ballah or Timsah, those names would have been used in the biblical text. The Hebrew term for the Sea of Reeds, *yam suph*, is the same term used in the Hebrew Bible for both the site of the crossing by the freed slaves and the location where the locusts were hurled. This term can also be found in other places in the Bible, including in Exodus 2:3, where Moses' mother placed him as a baby in a wicker basket and placed the basket "among the reeds by the bank of the Nile." However, like many other instances in the Bible, the text has to be read in context, because only in context can the meaning or intent of the biblical text become clear. Within the context of surrounding texts in Exodus, the Sea of Reeds where the locusts were hurled and the Sea of Reeds where the Israelites crossed were the same location.

In the last few centuries other sites have been offered up as the location of the biblical crossing of the Sea of Reeds. Because of earlier mistranslations of *yam suph*, the Red Sea has historically been thought of as the crossing site. The Red Sea between Egypt proper and the Sinai Peninsula was then as now too wide and too deep, and, as a salt sea, lacking in the marsh reeds or reeds of any kind to meet the criteria for the crossing site. The Bitter Lakes were also saltwater bodies, but because these lakes were shallow and were separated by a marsh, reeds and rushes grew around the lakes. Today reeds can be found along the shores of both lakes but especially between them in the marshes.

Lake Ballah and Lake Timsah, both north of the Bitter Lakes, have also been considered good candidates as possible crossing points. However, neither has the landscape to be confused for a sea (despite being marked as such on some ancient maps as discussed earlier in the book), nor is there a location within or between the lakes that could have been the site where the sea was parted. Both of these lakes were located well north in the delta and close to the Way of the Philistines and the defense forts Egypt located in this part of the wilderness to protect against invasion from Canaan. Figure 19 below shows the Way of the Philistines along the coast. This major route passed just south of Lake Timsah.

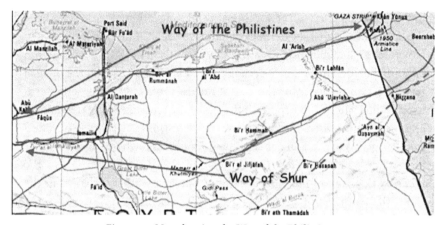

Figure 19: Map showing the Way of the Philistines.

When the Israelite's ancestors first settled in Egypt, it was in the eastern delta. At the time of the exodus anyone living in the delta would have been familiar with both of the delta's western of lakes, Ballah and Timsah (see Figure 20 below). Additionally, at the time of the exodus both Lake Timsah and Lake Ballah were connected to the Mediterranean Sea by man-made canals. Archaeologists have uncovered the ruins of connecting canals and "a harbor with quays where boats docked" according to Dr. James K. Hoffmeier.[56] He noted where Lake Ballah was "large enough to handle trading vessels" at the time of the exodus. Neither lake nor the water connections between them could have been the site of the Sea of Reeds crossing.

Those advocates for Mt. Sinai being located in the Arabian Desert of Saudi Arabia present a case for the Gulf of Aqaba being the Sea of Reeds. The Arabian Desert location for Mt. Sinai will be discussed later, but the Gulf of Aqaba was much too far away from Egypt to be a serious contender. The distance from the eastern delta departure area to the gulf is roughly 260 miles. This is well beyond any distance the Israelites could have travelled within forty-five days. Additionally, like the Red Sea, the Gulf of Aqaba was too deep and, as a saltwater body, it would have lacked the reeds associated with the biblical crossing point.

A likely reason for the Red Sea being the accepted translation for *yam suph* stems from the treatment of the term in the Greek Bible translation of the Old Testament, the Septuagint. The Septuagint was a very early translation dating to around the third century BCE, creating a Torah written in Koine Greek. The Greek translation equated *yam suph* with the Red Sea and because of this later translations and interpretations of the Torah adopted this relationship between the Hebrew term and Red Sea, including many if not most of the early Christian New Testament writings.

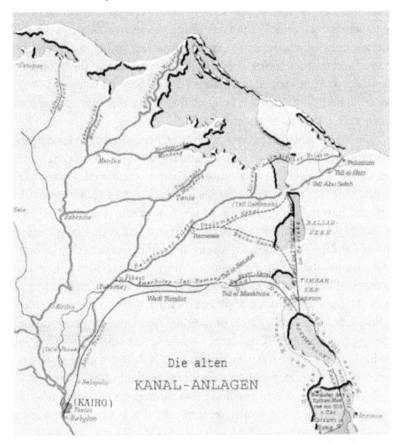

Figure 20: Map showing both Lake Timsah and Lake Ballah, referred to on the maps as seas. Courtesy of Dr. Gary Byers.

The Bitter Lakes were not seas. They were several shallow lakes and marshy areas located north of the Gulf of Suez. But they were large enough to be mistaken as seas to anyone seeing them for the first time. The marshy strip was very shallow and, despite being salty, would have had reeds growing along its shores. This connection between the lakes fit the image of the body of water filled with reeds that were parted for the Israelites to cross and then filled back in to destroy the chariots of pharaoh and pharaoh himself.

Today the Bitter Lakes are integral to the success of the Suez Canal and ships traversing the canal routinely anchor overnight in the lakes waiting the next day's routing through the canal in the direction they are going. At the time of the exodus the lakes were connected with the Gulf of Suez, a connection that was severed when the land rose sometime after the exodus, due to seismic activities.[57] The facts of the connection between the Bitter Lakes and the Gulf of Suez can be substantiated according to the geology of the areas and the rock formations at both Suez and around the Bitter Lakes. What has not been verified is the time frame when the lakes and the gulf were separated. Some scholars support the theory that this occurred after the exodus but this has not been verified.[58]

The sea crossing in the book of Exodus has been vexing for centuries. Early mistranslations of *yam suph* around the second or third century BCE have long contributed to this problem. In his *Antiquities*, Josephus also identified the *yam suph* as the Red Sea (*Antiquities* 2.15.3). This translation continued into the Common Era, where *yam suph* was recognized as the Red Sea in the Latin Vulgate as Mare Rubrum. And early English translations of the Bible, including the 1611 King James Version, continued this translation tradition. *Yam suph* appears in the Tanakh twenty-three times and many of these instances are not about the location of the parting and crossing of the sea in Exodus. Mentioned earlier, one refers to where Moses' mother placed him in the waters of the Nile. Another example of the use of *yam suph* comes from 1 Kings 9:26, where the text talks about King Solomon basing his navy on the *yam suph* near Eilat. Many of these instances of the use of *yam suph* are mentions of water sites that had no names.

It is very plausible to conclude that throughout the Bible whenever a body of water lacked a locally recognized name but had reeds growing on its shores, the term *yam suph* was used to describe it. Consider the two examples used herein; Moses was placed in the *yam suph* as a baby, a minor tributary without a name flowing through the eastern delta. And Solomon baseing his navy on the *yam suph* near Eilat may mean there was an inlet or protected shallow body of water along the edges of the Gulf of Aqaba where this occurred. The gulf is a saltwater body, but there are fresh water streams and wadis that flow into the gulf, and shallow marshy areas, one of which Solomon made use of.

Although a bit arcane, delving deeper into the translation of the original term for Sea of Reeds, the Hebrew for *suph* in *yam suph*, samach-vav-peh, can be read as either *suph* or *soph* depending on whether the vav is recognized as a *shuruk* (*suph*) or a cholam (*soph*). When the vav is read as *suph*, the words can translate to "sea of reeds" and when the vav is read as *soph* the translation refers to "distant sea" or "end of the sea." In Exodus 10:19 *yam suph* refers to where the eighth plague locusts were hurled to oblivion. It is also the term used later when the Israelites crossed the parted waters. In both cases the sea referred to could have been either the Distant Sea or the Sea of Reeds. It was unnamed and unknown to the Israelite host and looked like a sea both to Moses and the people.

Today the term Sea of Reeds is becoming more and more acceptable as the meaning for the Hebrew *yam suph*, סוּף-יָם. Considering the fact that the Sea of Reeds was not known to the Israelites and was located on the eastern edge of the wilderness between the Nile and the Bitter Lakes, it is very possible that the Hebrew term in this case may have been meant to read "distant sea." Describing the site of the biblical parting and crossing of the sea as a "distant sea" instead of the Sea of Reeds would not negate any of the reasons described in this chapter for the sea in question being the Bitter Lakes. On the contrary, referring to the sea of the biblical parting and crossing as the Distant Sea would add another supporting rationale for the crossing being the present-day Bitter Lakes.

17

Kadesh Barnea

These are the words that Moses spoke to all the Israelites across the Jordan in the wilderness in the Arabah opposite Suph between Paran and Tophel and Laban and Hazeroth and Di-Zahab, eleven days from Horeb by way of Mount Seir to Kadesh-Barnea.

—DEUTERONOMY 1:1

ONE ADDITIONAL SECTION OF text from the Bible should be considered to help identify where Mt. Sinai should be located. Deuteronomy 1:1–2 states that the Israelites traveled eleven days when they departed the area around Mt. Sinai to reach Kadesh Barnea in the northern Sinai. The assessment considered by this chapter from Table 1 addresses distance and geography. Based on the travel times and distances discussed earlier, the location of Mt. Sinai could not have been more than sixty to eighty miles from Kadesh Barnea. The location of Kadesh Barnea is not provided in the biblical text, however, there are two archaeological excavations, one at Ain el-Qadeis and the other at Ain el-Qudeirat, which are favored by archaeologists and scholars for Kadesh Barnea. Both of these sites are close to each other and are marked on the following map, Figure 21. The furthest distance the Israelites could have roughly traveled from Mt. Sinai to Kadesh Barnea is shown by the curve depicted on the map. Before presenting the conclusions of this book, it is worth considering the final alternative location proposed as Mt. Sinai, Hashem el-Tarif, in the eastern Sinai.

Figure 21: Map annotated by the author showing furthest distance
Israelites could have traveled from Kadesh Barnea to Mt. Sinai.

18

Hashem El-Tarif

Meanwhile, the LORD had said to Aaron, "Go and meet Moses in the wilderness." So he went and met Moses at the mountain of God and kissed him. 28 And Moses told Aaron everything the LORD had sent him to say, and all the signs He had commanded him to perform . . .

—EXODUS 4:27–28

EXODUS 4:27–28 IDENTIFIES THAT Mt. Sinai is in the otherwise imprecisely defined "wilderness." The final potential site for Mt. Sinai reviewed is Hashem el-Tarif. This mountain is a moderately high mountain for the Sinai that is more a plateau and is located not far from Bir Taba and the southeast border crossing between Egypt and Israel. This chapter provides assessment via scholarly input and biblical text as highlighted in Table 1, support by archaeology, geography, and distance, for considering this location to be Mt. Sinai.

A group of respected scholars and archaeologists

Figure 22: View of Hashem el-Tarif. Photo courtesy of photographer Mike Luddeni.

from the Associates for Biblical Research (ABR)[59] researched and followed a route from Egypt to Hashem el-Tarif in 2007. They believed the Israelites could have followed this route and this mountain was a viable candidate for Mt. Sinai. What the mountain looks like is shown in Figure 22. The location of the mountain is noted in Figure 23.

The team called their undertaking the Tarif Expedition (TE hereafter). The TE was challenged with travel restrictions that had been imposed by the Egyptian government around the time the expedition arrived, which remain in effect today. All non-official travel in the Sinai Peninsula was forbidden due in large part to the establishment of terrorist training camps by radical groups like ISIL (Islamic State in the Levant). These restrictions are in place today as they were in 2007. As a result, the TE has not published their work on this possible Mt. Sinai location, though a number of related articles have been published. They hope to conduct more intensive survey work on a return trip to the Sinai once the restrictions have been lifted.[60]

What was accomplished during the expedition by the team was to consider the biblical text as they traversed those areas of the Sinai Peninsula they could explore and evaluate. In their analysis, the TE interpreted the Bible's description of Moses' departure from Egypt after killing the Egyptian overseer as entering the desert of Shure and from there he would have taken a familiar route, such as a trade route, away from Egypt. This route led Moses to Midian and to the camp of Jethro after Moses beat back the male shepherds to allow Jethro's daughters to take water from the well.

According to TE, Midian was on the other side of the Sinai Peninsula approximately, 180 miles from northern Egypt.[61] The TE team recorded in their notes that Moses went west or north back towards Egypt, where he led the flock (of Jethro) to the western side of the desert and came to the Holy Mountain. Although the TE team did not explain the connection between Midian being 180 miles from northern Egypt and where the Holy Mountain was when Moses came to it, it is clear that they recognized that although Midian was much further from Egypt than Mt. Sinai, the mountain was on or near a route that was familiar to the Midianites and one that was regularly used by them as they traveled from pasture to pasture during the year.

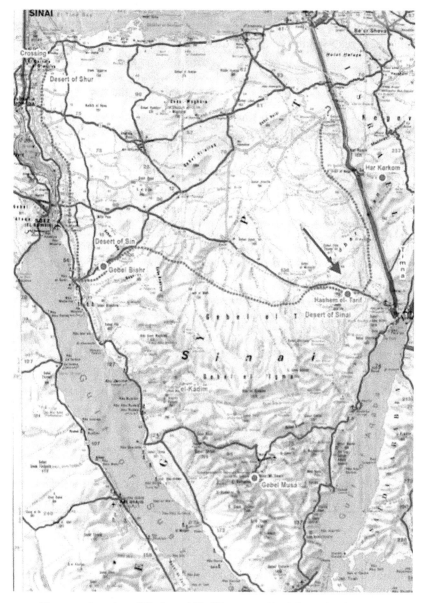

Figure 23: Location of Hashem el-Tarif in eastern Sinai shown by the arrow. Annotated map courtesy of photographer Mike Luddeni.

One thing the TE team was able to examine during their undertaking was the topography of Hashem el-Tarif. They witnessed the many prehistoric writings and cultic worship installations that were found and identified on the mountain as well as evidence of burials at Hashem el-Tarif. The conclusions reached were that these were evidence of the god of the Midianites and the desert peoples at the time being present on this mountain. It is why the mountain was a holy mountain.

According to Exodus 3:1, when Moses drove Jethro's flock, he came to Horeb (another name for Mt. Sinai), "the mountain of God." Being called "the mountain of God" in the Bible may have been an indication that this mountain was already considered a sacred place, which would be consistent with the identifications made by the TE team. "Mountain of God" may also have been anticipatory and written like this by Moses as he recorded the Five Books of Moses before his death. The latter possibility, that the mountain was considered a holy place when Moses arrived, gains credibility from an Egyptian fourteenth-century BCE inscription that refers to the land east of Egypt as "land of the nomads, Yahwe" or "and of the nomads who worship Yahwe."[62] However, the Egyptian inscription does not identify the place as holy to the Midianites; rather, it was holy because the nomads who worshiped Yahwe, the Israelites, made it holy. And the ancient Israelites did not leave cultic worship centers such as those found by the TE team on Hashem el-Tarif.

As noted earlier, Mt. Sinai was a presence on the historical stage of Abraham and his descendants only briefly in the Bible and, other than playing its role in Exodus and very briefly when Elijah sought sanctuary on its slopes, Mt. Sinai was intended to be forgotten according to ancient Jewish tradition. If the mountain were a holy place to nomads, Bedouin or Midianites or a combination of these, it would have been more than reasonable for the Bible to more clearly acknowledge this. That the Bible did not provides justification to question whether the evidence of cultic worship and burials on Hashem el-Tarif support the claim that it was the Mt. Sinai of the Bible. Additionally, God intended that Mt. Sinai be forgotten after the Israelites departed its location. If the mountain was a holy mountain to anyone, it would have been revisited long after the Israelite left.

The TE team addressed this in their notes, explaining that God may have decided to take the cultic mountain of the Midianites, which they thought was holy, and made it his Holy Mountain. Had God done this, it is reasonable to expect that the Bible would have made note of this fact. This would have been consistent with other text in the Bible where God was recorded as being superior to the false gods of ancient peoples or was recorded as being acknowledged by other people, non-Israelites, as being more powerful than their gods. That the Bible is silent on the extant holiness of the site raises questions about Hashem el-Tarif being Mt. Sinai.

The TE team was able to visit a number of places they believed were on the route the Israelites took. On the map included with the notes, the team marked where they believed the crossing of the Sea of Reeds took place. That map is Figure 23 above and the crossing was located well to the north of the Bitter Lakes and just north of where Lake Timsah was located. The notes do not explain why they concluded this was the location of the Sea of Reeds, the *yam suph,* but it is a location that has been accepted by other scholars as well. The possibility of the Sea of Reeds being located this far north in eastern Egypt was addressed earlier in this book: the location was too close to Egypt's eastern defenses and populated areas to have been the site of the crossing.

The Sea of Reeds had to be located beyond the wilderness that existed between the Nile River and the Bitter Lakes. The TE team did not address this but it would be an important point to get settled. The TE team went to Elim "where there were twelve springs and seventy palm trees, and they camped

Figure 24: One of the numerous wells that existed at the time of the exodus and today in the area called the Wells of Moses. Photo courtesy of photographer Mike Luddeni.

near the water" (the Gulf of Suez) (Exod 15:27). The author also visited the site the TE team called Elim. It is today called the Wells of Moses and most maps of the Sinai record it as such. The site very much looks like the Elim described in the Bible (see Figure 24 for a photo of just one area, showing a well and palm trees).

The TE team did not discuss travel times across distance as are discussed in this book. However, Dr. Bryant Wood, in an article published on the Associates for Biblical Research website in November 2008, did discuss travel times.[63] In the article Dr. Wood wrote the Israelites would have traveled each day approximately five to six miles, which is very consistent with the distance per day identified in this book. Wood determined the Israelites took sixty days to reach Sinai after leaving Egypt. He also took into account the Sabbaths during the march, when the Israelites following Moses would have rested, and concluded the total time on the march would have been fifty-two days. This time period would have been sufficient for the Israelites to journey from Rameses to Hashem el-Tarif if the journey took sixty days.

This book presents the view that the time it took to travel from Egypt to Mt. Sinai was forty-five days, a time frame that would not have enabled the Israelites to reach Hashem el-Tarif. Between the biblical texts of Exodus 19:1 and Numbers 33:3, discussed in detail earlier, the analysis offered provides compelling evidence for a travel time of forty-five days; indeed, that was the total time taken to reach Mt. Sinai but the Israelites actually advanced on their destination only thirty-seven days of that total. The area identified herein as the most likely place to find Mt. Sinai would have been close enough to Egypt for Moses and Aaron to travel and meet a number of times before the biblical meeting between Moses and pharaoh that ultimately resulted in the freeing of the slaves. This has all been discussed earlier in this book. Hashem el-Tarif is too far from Egypt, or from Rameses, to have supported the back-and-forth travel by Moses that the Bible records.

Dr. Wood and company plan to return to the Sinai to further their research. At that time it is likely travel and distance will be addressed or further refined by this talented team.

According to a map analysis, the distance from Hashem el-Tarif to the crossing point in the vicinity of Lake Timsah is approximately 192 miles. The distance from the mountain to the crossing site between the Bitter Lakes proposed in this book is approximately 152 miles. It would have taken the Israelites approximately 27–38 days to travel from the crossing site in the vicinity of Lake Timsah to Hashem el-Tarif. It would have taken between 21 to 30 days from the *yam suph* crossing in this book to Hashem el-Tarif. Add to these figures the time the Israelites traveled before they crossed the *yam suph*, and the Israelites could not have made the trip via either starting point to Hashem el-Tarif.

It would have been impossible for Moses and Aaron to have traveled from where pharaoh was to the Holy Mountain and back and forth as recorded in Exodus 2:15—6:28. The TE team did not specify where Moses and pharaoh met, though their notes allude to it being at Rameses, where the TE team saw the Israelites depart Egypt. This is consistent with views presented in this book on where the exodus began, provided Rameses was also the location of Avaris, the capital of the Hysos rulers of Egypt.

The TE team's notes suggested using Exodus 4:27 and some other text from the Bible to help refine where Mt. Sinai may have been located. The text in Exodus 4:27 says that Aaron met Moses at Mt. Sinai and kissed him. The TE team's notes concluded that Aaron had traveled from Egypt and Moses had traveled from Midian,[64] so they would have met along the Trans-Sinai Road. However, as explained earlier, Moses met with Aaron at Mt. Sinai. They met after Moses traveled to Egypt to visit his kin and, upon returning to Mt. Sinai, he met with Aaron, who had traveled from Egypt to meet him. They did not meet along any route; they met "at the mountain of God."

The TE team were not the only researchers of Hashem el-Tarif. Originally excavated by Professor Uzi Avner in 1982, both tombs and stone drawings were found on the mountain. Additionally, a number of open-air sanctuaries and small habitation sites were also found.[65] Professor Avner did not make arguments favoring this mountain being biblical Mt. Sinai. Professor Avner's records of his excavations and studies showed that one thing he determined was that the remains excavated on Hashem el-Tarif all date to the Late Neolothic Period and no Late Bronze Age remains were found. His view of these finds was that the age of the remains discounted Hashem el-Tarif as biblical Mt. Sinai.[66]

Another advocate for Hashem el-Tarif was Simcha Jacobovici, an adjunct professor from Huntington University. One reason the mountain met Jacobovici's expectations was that biblical Elim was located in the modern oasis of Ayun Musa, the Wells of Moses, or in this area. Elim had to be fourteen days from the mountain, so from Mt. Sinai Elim had to be 210 kilometers.[67] Jacobovici also said that Elim was just south of Lake Ballah. He said repeatedly in his article and in his web film *The Exodus Decoded* that it was vital to use the Bible to identify where Mt. Sinai was. In this case the Bible recorded that the Israelites traveled a three-days' journey in the Wilderness of Shur after crossing the Sea of Reeds. They then went to Elim and from there on to the Wilderness of Sin. According to Jacobovici's article and film, the location of Elim near Lake Ballah would have represented a backtracking back towards Egypt rather than the journey south and east that followed the crossing of the Sea of Reeds. Jacobovici also interpreted the biblical text to mean that the Israelites traveled fourteen days from Elim to Mt. Sinai.[68]

A careful reading of Exodus 16:1 places the Israelites between Elim and Sinai in the Wilderness of Sin on the forty-fifth day from Egypt, "on the fifteenth day of the second month after their departure from the land of Egypt." The Bible does not say where Elim was, only that it was somewhere from the Wilderness of Sin. From the Wilderness of Sin the Israelites traveled fifteen days to reach the Wilderness of Sinai and the Holy Mountain, according to Numbers 33:12–15. Elim was described in the Bible as being among wells, fresh water, and palm trees. The description in the Bible matches the geography of Wadi Garandel. Nothing near Lake Ballah comes close to matching this description.

Some of Professor Jacobovici's other explanations supporting Hashem el-Tarif being Mt. Sinai also appeared to be hard to substantiate. One more will be addressed. In his article Jacobovici used the United Nations High Commissioner for Refugees (UNHCR) estimates for how far a large group of refugees could move in a day to arrive at no more than fifteen kilometers. This is approximately nine miles per day.[69] His distance assumptions in both his articles and videos are based on this travel distance for modern refugees. As was noted in earlier in this book, the Israelites were a large group of freed slaves bringing with them babies and old people as well as flocks of animals. At best they would have traveled an average of six miles per day and often less than this, a point that Dr. Wood also made in his research. Additionally, the Israelites would have had to travel between water and pasturage locations so they would not have traveled in a straight line, further reducing how far they traveled each day. Refugees would have traveled under much different circumstances and been affected by different conditions. Jacobovici's assumptions were selective and biased to support his conclusions.

A map analysis can also help to assess the merits of Hashem el-Tarif being Mt. Sinai. Measuring distance on a map results in Hashem el-Tarif being approximately seventy-seven miles from Kadesh Barnea. Deuteronomy 1:2 says the Israelites traveled eleven days when they departed from Mt. Sinai to reach Kadesh Barnea. Based on the travel times explained in this book, the distance between these two sites would support Hashem el-Tarif being Mt. Sinai; the travel time frame is consistent. This route would have been through mostly barren desert and away from known travel routes. The point has been made that travelers did not digress from routes identified over centuries. Furthermore, this route of travel would have paralleled the western boundaries of the Promised Land. God forbid the Israelites from entering or seeing the Promised Land until the generation that left Egypt all died out. The possibility that the Israelites might have been able to see the Promised Land had they traveled from Hashem el-Tarif to Kadesh Barnea makes Hashem el-Tarif an unlikely candidate for Mt. Sinai.

The distance and time conclusions presented by the TE team and Professor Jacobovici raise questions about Hashem el-Tarif being Mt. Sinai that will have to be addressed in the future. Hashem el-Tarif cannot be discounted; a lot of excellent scholarship and research, as well as evidence on the ground, went in to the work done by the TE team and, to some extent, Professor Jacobovici. As the notes from the TE team record, "The precise location of Mt. Sinai is unknown."[70] Research and scholarship will continue to unlock this ancient mystery.

19

Pulling It All Together

On the third new moon of the Israelites' going out from Egypt,
on this day they came to the Wilderness of Sinai.

—EXODUS 19:1

JUST AS THE ISRAELITE trek to Mt. Sinai came to a conclusion, this analysis culminates in an epilogue. This book reflects an analysis of the biblical text regarding the evidence offered by the categories outlined in Table 1 of the first part of the exodus, from Egypt to Mt. Sinai. That analysis is based upon eight possible sites reviewed using eight key criteria presented in Table 1, reintroduced below.

It takes in to account the archaeology conducted to date, particularly archaeology of sites in the northeastern Nile Delta and around the salt lakes, which identify or attempt to identify sites recorded in the biblical text. The analysis was conducted in order to reach a conclusion on where it might be reasonable to search for the site of biblical Mt. Sinai.

A key premise of the research is that the Bible is a true and accurate historical record of the life and history of the family of Abraham and the ancient Israelite people. This book uses biblical text to narrow the area in which Mt. Sinai might be found. It further includes considerations derived from the geography of the area at the time of the exodus as well as recent and current archaeological excavations in the region where the exodus took place.

CRITERIA \\ PROPOSED SITES	Distance from Egypt <75-120 miles	Distance from Kadesh-Barnea	Supported by Bible text	Supported by archeology	Supported by geography	Supported by non-Biblical references	Supported by logistics considerations	Supported by scholars
Sweberg thesis	Yes	Yes	Yes	Yes	Yes	Yes	Yes	No
Jebel Musa (Hobbs)	No	No	No	Yes	No	Yes	Yes	Yes
Jebel Catherine	No	No	No	Yes	No	Yes	Yes	Yes
Jebel Serbal (Schneller)	No	No	No	Yes	No	Yes	Yes	Yes
Jebel al-Lawz (Whittaker)	No	No	No	No	No	No	No	No
Har Karkom (Anati)	No	Yes	No	No	No	No	No	Yes
Hashem el Tarif (TE Team)	No	Yes	Yes	No	Yes	No	No	Yes
Jebel Halal	No	Yes	No	No	No	No	No	No
Arif el Naka	No	Yes	No	No	No	No	No	No

Table 1: Analysis Results for Mt. Sinai Location

The exodus began in the region of Egypt called Rameses, within which lay the most fertile lands of Egypt at the time, which was ancient Goshen. This was the land granted by pharaoh to Joseph, who later was to be called Israel. The people who followed Jacob were the pre-Israelites who settled in Goshen during the rule of the Hyksos kings of Egypt. The Hyksos capital was in Avaris, located also in this area. When these kings were replaced by the Egyptian pharaohs of the Eighteenth Dynasty, the Israelite people were enslaved.

Throughout ancient Egypt's history the ruling families and high nobles built their summer palaces in the northeastern delta to take advantage of the mild breezes during the hot months of the year. These were common to the region thanks to the nearby Mediterranean Sea and the many tributaries of the Nile. Soon after Moses was born, he became a son of pharaoh's daughter. Her palace was located in the area of Canaan, near that of pharaoh's palace. This was the place Moses came to plea for the freedom of the slaves. It was here where the exodus began, in this region of Rameses, not the store city of Rameses.

The route the Israelites took, led by God, to Mt. Sinai, was not the most direct route. It did not go by way of the northern east-west travel route through the Sinai Peninsula, which was too dangerous for the newly freed slaves. Instead, God led the people south through the wasteland along the western side of the Bitter Lakes until they crossed the narrow waterway connecting the two lakes, the Reed Sea. The route then again went south until a point not far from present-day Wadi Garandel, at which time the Israelites went east until they came to Mt. Sinai.

It took the Israelites forty-five days to reach Mt. Sinai from Egypt. But because of stops for the Sabbath, a day lost fighting the Amalekites, and a day when God directed them back on their route, they actually traveled thirty-seven days before arriving at Mt. Sinai. Their speed and distance traveled each day was limited due to the numbers of people in the host, which included old people, very young children, and herds and flocks that needed to be fed, watered, and rested. They could not travel in a straight path but had to follow a course that brought them to water sources and grazing sources.

Before reaching Mt. Sinai, the Israelites arrived at Elim. There is no archaeological or extant evidence identifying the location of Elim. However, the Bible offers a very clear description of the surroundings and this description offers a very clear idea of Elim's location. Elim was located in a place where both plentiful palm trees and a dozen springs were located. This biblical description of Elim is a key description of where the Israelites were, even though Elim has, to date, not been discovered. There is no other place in the western Sinai that matches the description offered by the Bible for Elim other than Wadi Garandel. From this location Mt. Sinai was twelve to fifteen days' distance.

Considering the route, rate of travel, and time of travel from Egypt, along with the route, rate of travel, and time of travel from Mt. Sinai to Kadesh Barnea, biblical Mt. Sinai should be sought in the area of the Sinai generally east of Port Suez and among the chain of mountains running the length of the western side of the peninsula.

Some of these mountains lack the water and pasturage that the Israelites would have needed during their stay at Mt. Sinai. But several do satisfy the requirements.

There is one mountain that does fit the requirements to be Mt. Sinai. That mountain is Bashar Shin, or Jebel Bishr. On some maps the mountain is called Jebel Sin Bisher. The name Jebel Bishr will be used hereafter. The location of the mountain is identified in Figure 25.

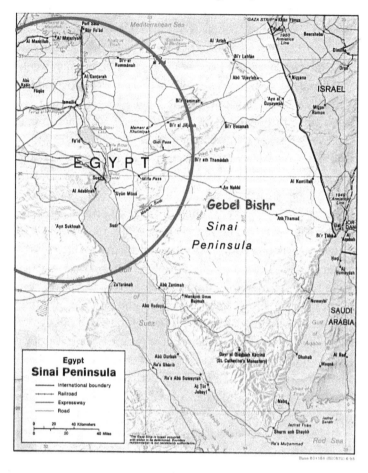

Figure 25: Depicted on the map are the location of Jebel Bishr and the radius distance the Israelites traveled in thirty-nine days from Memphis, Egypt. Map given to author when a member of the MFO.

Jebel Bishr is within the range that the Israelites would have traveled both from Rephidim and from their start location in Rameses when Moses parted from pharaoh after the king finally agreed to free the slaves. Jebel Bishr is roughly three days from Avaris by chariot, indicating that Moses was being honest with pharaoh when he asked that pharaoh allow the Israelite slaves to travel for three days so that they could sacrifice to the Lord, as the text reads in Exodus 3:18. Jebel Bishr is not a particularly tall mountain, reaching a height of 2,657 meters, or 8,715.

The ancient Jewish sages, as noted earlier, believed that Mt. Sinai was neither tall nor imposing, so the stature of Jebel Bishr meets the Bible's description. Open, level terrain surrounds the mountain on three sides, especially the southern side. This area would have easily accommodated the Israelites encamped at the base of the mountain as described in the Bible. The mountain overlooks Wadi Sudr, a watercourse that holds standing water when rain falls in the Sinai and a location where more water was present in ancient times than is present today.

Although this area of Wadi Sudr could not sustain a very large population for an extended period of time today, around 1200–1440 BCE, roughly the time period when the exodus occurred,[71] water was more prevalent in the area both in terms of annual rainfall and fossil groundwater.[72] It is also reasonable to accept that the Israelites had sufficient water because Wadi Sudr was not far from the best-watered site in the Sinai, already described, Wadi Gharandel. There were a number of wells at this site in ancient times.

Water flows in the area from east to west, even beneath the surface, so water from Wadi Sudr flowed to the Gulf of Suez. The water in and below the wadi is potable water and not brackish as is the case in many other places in the Sinai. This is possible because seawater in this area does not flow from the Gulf of Suez under the western border of the Sinai to create brackish water. Today there is vegetation growing in the wadi and it was more abundant in ancient times.

There is a fossil water aquifer beneath this area of the Sinai that can be reached by digging wells. There are approximately thirty-five productive wells in the western area of Wadi Sudr in the vicinity of Jebel Bishr.[73] The Bible records that the population remained in the vicinity of Mt. Sinai for an extended period of time, enough for Moses to get the Ten Commandment tablets from God, destroy them when the people built the golden calf, and then spend forty days and nights reproducing the tablets afterwards. At no time does the Bible record the Israelites having any water difficulties while sojourning in the Wilderness of Sinai. There was either enough or God provided as he so often did during the exodus.

Earlier the book discussed one other site that is important in determining the location of Mt. Sinai. The location is Kadesh Barnea, which Deuteronomy 1:2 says is eleven days' travel from Mt. Sinai (Horeb). Based on this, Mt. Sinai had to be no more than eighty to one hundred miles from Kadesh Barnea. Jebel Bishr is roughly seventy-two to ninety-six miles from the location for Kadesh Barnea. According to the travel times and distances, Jebel Bishr does satisfy the text of Deuteronomy. The distance from Kadesh Barnea to Mt. Sinai is depicted in Figure 21, in chapter 17.

Jebel Bishr is located well north of the ancient Egyptian mining site of Serabit el-Khadim and very well south of the Way of the Philistines. This location minimized the risk of encountering any Egyptian military presence during their travels from Egypt to Mt. Sinai.

It is impossible to declare with absolute certainty which mountain in the Middle East is the site of biblical Mt. Sinai. Jebel Bishr or any of the modest mountains that surround it satisfy the requirements for where Mt. Sinai had to be located based on the biblical text and considering the facts of travel time for a large body of humans and animals and the environment surrounding Mt. Sinai. Jebel Bishr is a more likely candidate than most. Considering the description of the mountain as not imposing, nor the highest in the Sinai, and taking into account how far and how long the Israelites traveled to get to Mt. Sinai, Jebel Bishr is the best candidate to be Mt. Sinai. Figure 26 shows a route from Goshen to Mt. Sinai with the start beginning at Rameses and ending at Jebel Bishr.

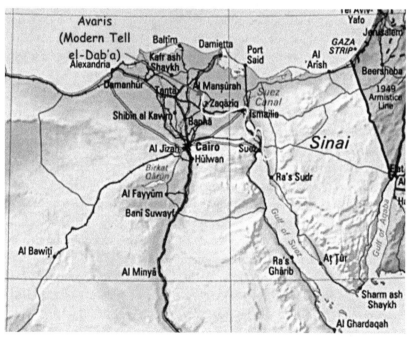

Figure 26: Route taken by Israelis from Avaris, Goshen, to Jebel Bishr, depicted by the white squiggly line.

Figure 27: View of Jebel Bishr from Wadi Sudr.
Photo courtesy of photographer Mike Luddeni.

There was a steady supply of water and pasturage available during each season in the desert in the area around Jebel Bishr. Figure 27 above depicts a current view of Jebel Bishr. There is both chalk and flint along the flanks of the mountain and Exodus 4:25 records where Zipporah, Moses' wife, used a flint to circumcise her son during her encounter with God. The family was traveling to Egypt from Mt. Sinai to meet Moses' kin and it is reasonable that Zipporah took advantage of the flint available on the mountain to fashion the knife she used.

Jebel Bishr does not have any evidence of ancient graves or pagan holy sites but a number of adjacent mountains have one or both of these. This mountain does have a number of caves along its sides, which Elijah could have hidden in if this is Mt. Sinai.

Figure 16 in chapter 15 depicts the distance the Israelites traveled from Elim to Mt. Sinai. Figure 21 in chapter 17 depicts the distance from Kadesh Barnea that Mt. Sinai had to be. Putting the two maps together provides a map depiction of the area in the Sinai Peninsula where Mt. Sinai was and is. Figure 28 below shows this area. The area depicted lies along the mountain spine of the peninsula and Gebel Bishr, along with a number of small mountains near Gebel Bishr, is in the right area to be biblical Mt. Sinai.

The Bible is the only reference of any kind available that talks about Mt. Sinai. The Bible was and is the factual history of the family of Abraham and the Israelite people. It is factual in the context of the understanding of history at the time. Originally the Bible was an oral record, which later came to be a written history. The Bible does not provide a comprehensive description of where Mt. Sinai is. This is to be expected. God told the Israelite people that the mountain was death to anyone who ventured upon it. Clearly God wanted the mountain to be forgotten. So the references to it are intentionally scant in the Bible. However, as this book has shown, the evidence is sufficient to narrow the focus on where Mt. Sinai has to be.

We know from physical evidence how fast and how far a large group of people traveling with young children, very old people, and flocks and herds of animals would have traveled each day in this harsh environment. We have evidence of where the Israelites departed from Egypt. We know where they did not travel, with God's guidance, to avoid encounters with Egyptians. We have a very good idea how far Mt. Sinai was from Kadesh Barnea near the border to the Promised Land. Lastly, although we do not know where most of the places are that the Israelites rested each day, we have a very good idea where one critical site was located, that of Elim, which was near the end of the journey from Egypt to the Holy Mountain. With all this evidence we can conclude that Mt. Sinai was not in the southern Sinai mountains. It was not beyond the borders of the Sinai Peninsula in the Arabian Desert or inside the boundaries of the Promised Land. There is one area only where Mt. Sinai has to be and this area is depicted in Figure 28. This area is along the mountain chain that stretches from northwestern Sinai down to the southern tip of the peninsula and is roughly east of today's Port Suez. There are a number of modest mountains in this area that could be Mt. Sinai. The best candidate for the reasons stated is the mountain Gebel Bishr, located due east of today's Port Suez.

What comes next? As archaeologists continue to excavate ancient sites uncovered in present-day Egypt, including the Sinai Peninsula, it is hoped and likely that places preserved in the biblical text will be discovered and these will bring to light further evidence that supports or refutes the evidence presented in this book.

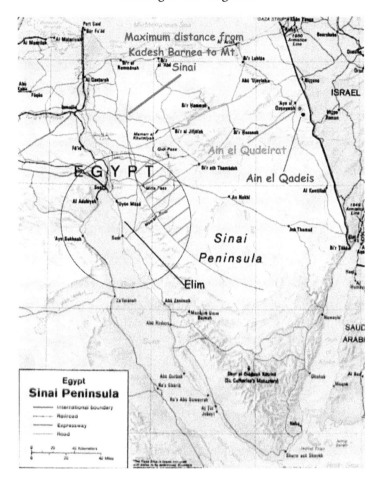

Figure 28: Map showing area in which author believes Mt. Sinai is located,
highlighted by parallel lines.

Epilogue

Identity of Pharaoh of Exodus

The Lord instructed Moses, "When you go back to Egypt, see that you perform before pharaoh all the wonders that I have put within your power. But I will harden his heart so that he will not let the people go."

—EXODUS 4:21

IN A DISCUSSION ABOUT where Mt. Sinai is located the pharaoh who was engaged by Moses is not a relevant discussion topic. As the assessment biblical and scholarly texts, geography, and archaeology via Table 1 concluded, who the pharaoh was has no impact on where Mt. Sinai is located. In fact, the identity of the pharaoh has eluded centuries of scholars and researchers and continues to be a topic of much debate. I am including this chapter because the topic is of interest and because I have reached my own conclusions about the subject. I hope this chapter becomes a point of interest to those reading this book.

There are a number of possible pharaohs based on evidence and facts that support arguments favoring each of them. To date there is no evidence clearly linking any specific pharaoh to the exodus. The exodus can be dated to have occurred sometime between 1200 and 1400 BCE. To get more precise than this becomes much more problematic as most scholars fall into one of two camps, arguing for either an early date of the exodus or a late date for the exodus. Those favoring an early date can make a case for the exodus occurring around 1446 BCE. Those favoring a late date make an equally compelling case for the exodus taking place around 1270 BCE.

Although in the past many pharaohs had their champions among scholars, in more recent times a general acceptance that the pharaoh in question is most probably one of the early Eighteenth Dynasty pharaohs has become more prevalent. Cecil B. DeMills's classic motion picture *The Ten Commandments* offered the view that Rameses was pharaoh at the time, reflecting the prevailing view when the movie came out. This has been discounted as Rameses ruled long after the exodus took place, regardless of whether it was during a later or earlier date. The difference between the early and late dates is two centuries, a wide discrepancy. Until the rise of the Egyptian monarchy period, scholars have been challenged to correlate ancient dates with the modern western calendar.

Attempts to identify the right pharaoh have been complicated by the way ancient Egyptians recorded events. Surviving Egyptian records for the most part are propagandistic and intended to highlight the accomplishments of pharaohs or their godhood. Dating was based on the regnal years of the pharaohs and lacked the precision we have come to accept in modern times. Writing was believed to be sacred; anything written and recorded supported the reality of the event or person.

Ancient Egyptians believed that any event that was not recorded never happened.[74] In that light, the ancient Egyptians never recorded anything that did not honor or glorify the pharaoh or Egypt. By not doing so, the event or person, it was believed, never existed or took place. Over time the person or event became lost to history. Pharaohs that fell out of favor had their monuments and records destroyed and statues defaced. By such means these pharaohs ceased to be as their histories were stricken from the memories of the people.

A good historical example of this tendency to erase bad news was Akhenaten. Akhenaten began his reign as Amenhotep IV but changed his name to Akhenaten when he introduced a new worship of just one god, Aten. In doing so the pharaoh eschewed the system of beliefs in multiple gods and, at the same time, he closed all the temples of these other gods and kicked out their priests. When Akhenaten died the priests returned and restored the old gods, returned to the ways of the past before Akhenaten, and tried to wipe the memory of Akhenaten from history, destroying his monuments, temples, and statues and removing his name from the king lists.

Fortunately, enough evidence did survive enabling scholars and archaeologists to learn of this pharaoh and search for evidence of his tomb. When Bible critics point out that no evidence of the exodus has ever been found in Egyptian records, this is a case of an event that did not favorably shed light on Egypt and so it was never recorded. As Dr. Bryant Wood noted in his fall 2008 article on the exodus, the "absence of evidence is not evidence of absence."[75]

The Bible always refers to the ruler of Egypt as "pharaoh." The throne name was never used. This was consistent with Egyptian historiography. During the Old Kingdom era of Egypt, the word *pharaoh* meant "great house" and it was used to refer to the royal palace. During the Ramesside period the term pharaoh was used in lieu of the actual name of the pharaoh. Hoffmeier stated, "From its inception until the tenth century BCE, the term 'pharaoh' stood alone, without juxtaposed personal name. In subsequent periods, the name of the monarch was generally added on."[76]

The reason the name of the pharaoh of the exodus is not present within the text of the Bible is more because such omission reflected the standard practice of the day in ancient Egypt. Indeed, for many scholars this fact is evidence of the historicity of the Bible and proof that the book of Exodus was written long before King David's time. Moses was raised as a well-educated Egyptian; he would have written in a manner reflecting his times. This is also why other pharaohs in the Five Books of Moses were also not named, even the "good pharaoh" in Genesis 47:7, whom Joseph served and Jacob blessed. This was the contemporary custom that a prince of Egypt, which Moses was, would have practiced.

According to Hoffmeier, there may be another reason pharaoh's throne name is absent in the Bible. "Theological reasons" may have had more to do with pharaoh's throne name being absent. The Bible was written not to explain who the pharaoh of the exodus was; the text was intended to clarify for Israel who God was and what his role was during the exodus and his relationship with the Israelite people.[77] To put the point on it, in the history of the Israelite nation, the identity of pharaoh was simply not of importance.

Dr. Steven Collins, in his excellent book on the subject of the pharaoh of the exodus, *Let My People Go!*, took a very effective approach to the challenge of identifying the pharaoh by focusing on historical synchronisms. Dr. Collins used historical synchronism to narrow the field of potential candidates for the pharaoh of the exodus. The choices offered in the book are Tuthmosis III, Amenhotep II, Tuthmosis IV, Amenhotep III and Akhenaten, all early Eighteenth Dynasty rulers.

Studying and analyzing ancient history, especially history of nations like the Egyptians who dated according to the regnal times of kings, can be very challenging. This is especially true when seeking to reconcile the biblical accounts with Egyptian history. Virtually nothing seems to synchronize.[78] Using a method like historical synchronism can be effective because this method can be used to find historical event patterns that correlate events from both "relevant biblical and Egyptian materials."[79] As Dr. Collins pointed out in his book, this kind of approach is useful because it can correlate events from the exodus that are considered positive from the Israelite point of view with events from the same time period that would be considered negative from the Egyptian point of view.

It was noted earlier that Egyptians did not record for history events that placed either the pharaoh or Egypt in a negative light. Historical synchronism can be used when there is not a clearly identified negative event but there is historical evidence of the implications of such an event, such as economic hardship resulting from the death of a pharaoh and destruction of his army. As Dr. Collins stated, "The Egyptians would never admit to the kinds of events described in the book of Exodus."[80] It is not often that scholars have applied the concepts of historical synchronism; it is, nevertheless, a valuable tool for making sense of historical pictures where very little information is actually available.

In *Let My People Go!* historical synchronism is used to identify the likely pharaoh of the exodus by understanding the impact of the events of the exodus on Egypt. Clearly, when added together, the events leading up to the exodus, the beginning of the exodus, and the devastation to the army at the Sea of Reeds would have had calamitous effects on Egypt. As a result of the events of the exodus, a significant component of Egypt's economic capabilities was removed as many if not all of the slaves contributing to the economic well-being of the nation were removed by being set free.

The Bible really only focuses on the Israelite slaves, though other enslaved people who were not Israelite probably left with the Israelites to follow Moses. There is nothing in the Bible or in Egyptian history to indicate that any non-Israelite slaves remained in Egypt after the exodus took place. Regardless, the departure of the Israelites would have had a devastating impact on the Egyptian economy.

Before pharaoh agreed to free the slaves and the exodus began, Egypt was struck by the ten plagues. The Bible does not clearly say how long the plagues lasted; it could have been days, weeks, or even years. Certainly each plague lasted more than just a day or few days. Too short a period of time and their effect would not have impacted on the Egyptian population or impressed pharaoh. Collectively, the effects of the plagues would have had a significant impact on the nation and its people.

By the tenth plague, all of Egypt would have suffered severe economic trauma and the economy would have certainly been in significant stress. Additionally, the emotional psyche of the population would have been seriously impacted in a very negative way. Things would not have improved when pharaoh finally freed the Israelites. As the Bible makes very clear in Exodus 12:35–36, "The Israelites had done Moses' bidding and borrowed from the Egyptians objects of silver and gold, and clothing. And the Lord disposed the Egyptians favorably toward the people, and they let them have their request; thus they stripped the Egyptians." Egypt was a rich and prosperous nation and now it was "stripped" of its wealth. The economy took a devastating hit from the departing Israelites on top of the damage already caused by the plagues.

The Bible next records what occurred at the Sea of Reeds. Pharaoh had a change of heart as God once again hardened it and he pursued the fleeing former slaves, leading from his own chariot an army of six hundred of the best chariots (Exod 14:7–9). The elite chariot force of the army was drowned and likely pharaoh with it. The book of Exodus infers but does not specifically state that pharaoh died in the Sea of Reeds, but Psalm 136 clearly states that both pharaoh and his army were drowned in the sea.

Instead of looking for nonbiblical evidence for the exodus, *Let My People Go!* considers the health of the economy and foreign affairs of the nation during the time of the early pharaohs of the Eighteenth Dynasty to find the evidence of how the events of the exodus impacted these health indicators to determine who was the most likely pharaoh at the time of the exodus. Because the Egyptian sources were, as noted earlier, very propagandistic and intended to support political and religious agendas, they were not good sources to help in the identification.

Based on the analysis of the impact of the ten plagues and the destruction of the Egyptian army and pharaoh, Dr. Collins concluded that Tuthmosis IV was the most likely pharaoh of the exodus. Dr. Collins made the case for Tuthmosis IV based on events affecting Egypt in a way that would have been consistent with unexplained events in Egypt's history directly causing the beginning of a sharp decline in Egypt's strength at a time when that strength was at its height.

Reflecting the complexity of Egyptian history and the challenges faced in determining who ruled when, it is possible to reach another conclusion of who was pharaoh at the time of the exodus also using historical synchronism. Tuthmosis IV was succeeded by his son Amenhotep III. Amenhotep III was the ninth pharaoh of the Eighteenth Dynasty. He ruled Egypt when it was at the height of its power. He maintained extensive diplomatic contacts with other nations. His reign is noted for having been a time of peace over the course of thirty-eight years. His reign would not have been as peaceful if his father had been the pharaoh of the exodus and its associated upheavals, raising the possibility that another pharaoh may have been the exodus pharaoh. Akhenaten succeeded Amenhotep III.

Using historical synchronism as a basis for analysis, it is possible to consider Akhenaten as the likely pharaoh of the exodus. By the time of the exodus, the Israelite slaves were located throughout Egypt, not just in the northeast Nile Delta, though their concentration would have been highest in this region. As was noted earlier, the Israelites who settled in Goshen with Joseph "were fertile and prolific"; their population increased rapidly and the "land was filled with them." Now they were reduced to slaves and they labored at all kinds of work in the fields and at hard labor in brick and mortar (Exod 1:8–14). However, the primary role for the slaves was centered on the building projects intended to reflect the glory and magnificence of pharaoh. The Bible records that the primary labor of the slaves was work on constructions made using mud bricks.

When Moses first confronted pharaoh and asked him to free the slaves in Exodus 5, pharaoh responded by ordering his taskmasters to stop providing straw for making mud bricks and insisting the slaves maintain their quota of bricks. It is clear from the narrative of Exodus 5 that making and applying mud bricks was the major task for the slaves in Egypt, certainly for those tasks prescribed by pharaoh. When denied the straw needed to make bricks, the Bible says the people "scattered throughout the land of Egypt to gather stubble for straw" (Exod 5:12). "Throughout the land" means the slaves went well beyond the area of the Nile Delta in their efforts to find straw or suitable substitutes for it.

The slaves were clearly working on a major building project. One project that has been suggested for employing significant numbers of slaves was the construction of the two grain cities of Pithom and Rameses. These would have been major projects suitable to occupy a very large number of slaves, however, these grain cities could not have been the projects because, according to the Bible, these cities were already built by the time of Moses as recorded in Exodus 1:11: "they *built* garrison cities [store cities] for pharaoh: Pithom and Rameses" (emphasis added). These cities were not the project; the slaves had already built these cities in the past. Now the slaves were tasked with another major undertaking occupying their efforts as required by pharaoh.

Ancient Egyptian history offers a possible answer to what the project was and also offers a possible answer to who the pharaoh of the exodus was. The pharaoh was Akhenetan.

Stephen Rosenberg from the W.F. Albright Institute of Archaeological Research in Jerusalem wrote an article in the *Jerusalem Post* in 2014 proposing Tutankhamun as the pharaoh of the exodus. Although there are a number of reasons not to consider Tutankhamun as the pharaoh of the exodus, in the article Rosenberg offered a compelling explanation of the project the Israelite slaves were engaged on at the time of Moses.[81] That project was building the new capital city of Amarna. Amarna was the capital for only one pharaoh: Akhenaten.

The Israelites worked in mud brick, they were semi-skilled, and they were working on a project requiring thousands of workers. Temples and palaces were built of shaped stones. This is a skill not referenced in the Bible, so the Israelite slaves did not work on stone construction. Stone construction required skilled workers above the capabilities of slaves.

When pharaoh freed the slaves, it was at a time or period of turmoil during which the ten plagues had devastated Egypt. Although the Egyptians would not have recorded for history the freeing of this large slave population, it would have been impossible to hide major turmoil impacting the well-being and security of the entire nation. This was a time of economic crisis in Egypt, which corresponds to the time during the rule of Akhenaten.

Pharaoh Akhenaten assumed the throne following the death of Amenhotep III, around 1382 BCE. Akhenaten was known as Amenhotep IV until the fifth year of his reign, when he changed his name to Akhenaten, showing his allegiance to Aten, the sun god. He ruled for seventeen years, during which time he moved the royal capitol to Amarna, where he built a new city intended to be the lasting center of worship of Aten. It was not to be, as the worship of Aten gave way to the return of the many traditional gods of Egypt upon his death. Akhenaten's city in Amarna was located on the Nile River roughly 186 miles north from the traditional seat of power for the rest of the pharaohs of the Eighteenth dynasty, Thebes.

The building of Amarna was the major project the Israelite slaves were working on. Historically, none of the early Eighteenth Dynasty pharaohs undertook any projects as profound or labor intensive as this, an entire city. The pharaoh was determined to have his new capitol built as quickly as possible. Thus, he would have put the majority of his slaves to work on it. Everything was built in mud brick in the beginning. According to history, the city was built in a very short period of time and it was built entirely of mud brick. Only the temple to Aten and the palace of pharaoh were to be built of traditional stone and were thus not finished during this time.[82] The location of the new city was on the east bank of the Nile. There was plenty of soft mud, thanks to the annual flooding of the Nile, but there was little straw available.

The Bible records that the slaves were required to make mud bricks without being provided with essential straw (Exod 5:7). Clearly this was provided for the manufacture of mud bricks, until the Bible records that pharaoh ordered that the straw stop being provided. Since straw was available in the delta due to the agriculture present there, but not available in the vicinity of Amarna, which was in a more barren part of Egypt, this had to be the project the slaves were all dedicated to, as they spread throughout the land to find the necessary straw or straw equivalents for the bricks.

During this time of the Eighteenth Dynasty there were no other major projects anywhere in Egypt that would have required the millions of mud bricks or the vast army of slaves to make and use them for the project. Amarna was the source of the oppression and "forced labor" (Exod 1:11) that God heard and decided to act upon. The project would have created a major drain on the wealth of the kingdom, already strained for a number of economic reasons, including the loss of revenue from the temples when Akhenaten closed them and rejected the priests of all the gods other than Aten.

The rejection of the host of gods of Egypt by the pharaoh in favor of Aten along with the associated upheaval in the priesthood and closure of temples throughout Egypt would have been a significant disruption in the nation's society and ability to collect taxes and revenue. As Egypt was dealing with all of this, Akhenaten's untimely death and the restoration of the old gods would have created significant further upheaval exacerbating the problems the country was already facing due to the loss of former imperial holdings and vassals.[83] And, of course, there was the devastating impact on the economy and state caused by the ten plagues, as discussed earlier. By the time Akhenaten assumed the throne, the state had already started to decline, having lost a number of imperial holdings and seeing much of the treasury obliterated by unwise decisions by previous pharaohs.[84]

After the tenth plague, the death of the firstborn in Egypt, the slaves were freed to leave Egypt. Akhenaten was probably not in Amarna meeting with Moses, nor is this where he finally agreed to free the slaves. The temple and the palace were not yet built in Amarna, so it was very unlikely that pharaoh was there. Pharaoh was in residence in one of his palaces in the eastern delta of the Nile. This was where Moses met with pharaoh and it was also where Moses was raised. The palace where pharaoh was temporarily living and ruling from was either the same palace his daughter, Moses' stepmother, the princess, resided at or a palace close by. Neither the Bible nor ancient Egyptian history tell where Moses met with the pharaoh, or where pharaoh was when he released the slaves. This is a reasonable case that can be made if Akhenaten was the pharaoh at the time of Moses.

It is probable that Moses was born near the palace and as a baby was placed by his mother into the waterproof wicker basket and set into the waters of the Nile. He drifted with the current as his sister watched from the shores to see what would "befall him" (Exod 2:4). He was found by the "daughter of pharaoh" (2:3), who made him her son and named him Moses because she "drew him out of the water" (2:10). Once Moses was placed in the royal family by his stepmother, the "daughter of pharaoh," he would have been raised as a royal son and he would have been educated along with other royal children.

Moses' family would have resided close to this palace, which answers the question of where Moses traveled to when he traveled back and forth from Mt. Sinai to visit his kin (Exod 4:18) and when he met with the Israelite elders and his older brother Aaron. His family lived in Goshen. This area, where a number of pharaonic palaces were built, is also located seventy-five miles from present-day Ismaelia. Ismaelia was just north of the Bitter Lakes and is an ancient starting point for travelers entering the Sinai desert or going north to meet the Way of the Philistines or, as it was known to the ancient Egyptians, the Way of Horus, which ran along the Mediterranean coast to Gaza. This was a very important Egyptian region.

Unless and until more evidence is uncovered, it is unlikely that we will definitively know who the pharaoh of the exodus was. The above narrative offers reasons to consider two early Eighteenth Dynasty pharaohs as possible choices. And while the pharaoh is not vital to the search for biblical Mt. Sinai, scholars and historians will continue to look for clues identifying who that pharaoh was.

Endnotes

1. From the Midrash, the set of Rabbinic literature containing the early interpretations and commentaries on the Torah and oral histories. Humbleness of Sinai taken from Chabad.org, "Why Mount Sinai?"

2. On November 15, 2011, this author had a discussion with renowned American rabbi Dr. David Wolpe. We discussed this as being the most likely outcome if Mt. Sinai was known or if the burial place of Moses were known.

3. Hoffmeier, *Israel in Egypt*, 63.

4. MacDonald, "Land of Goshen in Egypt," 55.

5. Gertoux, "Moses and the Exodus," 22.

6. Gertoux, "Moses and the Exodus," 22.

7. Gertoux, "Moses and the Exodus," 22.

8. During the period of 1994–1996 the author conducted numerous explorations to find these forts. The two found are clearly of Roman design, both retaining most of the fortifications, and while one has two standing courtyard columns the other boasted all four that were originally erected. These forts lack sufficient importance to warrant excavation by anyone, but the author found numerous Roman coins and a plethora of pottery remains, including two unbroken clay oil lamps and an unbroken clay storage carafe. All finds were on the surface or partially exposed as in the case of the lamps and carafe.

9. In 1988 the author was caught in a four-hour sandstorm in central Sinai. When it was over, the vehicle he was in had no paint on the front of the truck and the license plate was a smooth rectangle of aluminum; all vestiges of paint had been removed. The vehicle was a Jeep Grand Wagoneer.

10. Beitzel, *Moody Atlas of Bible Lands*, 91.

11. Bradford, *Arrow, Sword and Spear*, 24.

12. Conder, *Palestine Exploration Fund Quarterly Statement 1883*, 79–90.

13. Kitchen, *On the Reliability of the Old Testament*, 264.

14. Egyptologists tend to dodge the issue of population numbers, as there are no statistics available and all such numbers are based on more or less educated guesswork:

- Edward S. Ellis put the New Kingdom population at 5 million.

- The author of the Royal Ontario Museum website gives an estimate of between 1.5 and 5 million Egyptians during the Pyramid Age, a rather non-committing number for a nicely vague and long time period.

- Dominic Rathbone estimates that Roman Egypt had a population of 3–5 million, and Bagnall and Frier (reshafim.org) concur.

- According to the Harris papyrus, somewhat in excess of 100,000 people belonged to the temple estates during the reign of Ramses III. James Henry Breasted thought that they had been less than 2 percent of the population, which would give an upper limit of 5,000,000 towards the end of the New Kingdom.

15. Janzen, "Ancient Egyptian Population Estimates," lines 8–13.

16. Kitchen, *On the Reliability of the Old Testament*, 264.

17. Kitchen, *On the Reliability of the Old Testament*, 264.

18. Kitchen, *On the Reliability of the Old Testament*, 264.

19. Kitchen, *On the Reliability of the Old Testament*, 265.

20. Kitchen, *On the Reliability of the Old Testament*, 265. All references to individuals working out population models in this paragraph comes from this page in Kitchen.

21. Berlin and Brettler, *Jewish Study Bible*, margin notes for Exod 3:1.

22. Note, from Exodus 6:1 up to this verse God had only been speaking with Moses.

23. Hobbs, *Mount Sinai*, 68.

24. Hobbs, *Mount Sinai*, 68.

25. Father Michael told this author this during one of many meetings at the monastery in 1989.

26. Hobbs, *Mount Sinai*, 35–36.

27. Hobbs, *Mount Sinai*, 42.

28. Hobbs, *Mount Sinai*, 42.

29. Hobbs, *Mount Sinai*, 45–48

30. Hobbs, *Mount Sinai*, 49.

31. Hobbs, *Mount Sinai*, 51.

32. Schneller, *Durch die Wueste zum Sinai*, 189.

33. Hobbs, *Mount Sinai*, 69.

34. Hobbs, *Mount Sinai*, 69.

35. Hobbs, *Mount Sinai*, 52–53.

36. Hobbs, *Mount Sinai*, 68–72.

37. Bradford, *With Arrow, Sword and Spear*, 24.

38. Three separate Bedouin chiefs in Sinai, from the tribes of the Gbaliyyah near Mt. St. Catherines, the Sawarkah near El Arish in northeast Sinai, and the Mzenah near El Tur along the Red Sea coast, told this author they carried their tribal name when they moved their herds. The Sawarkah travelled annually to the western side of the Suez and the Mzenah and Gbaliyyah annually traveled into Saudi Arabia.

39. Davies, *Way of the Wilderness*, 64.

40. Davies, *Way of the Wilderness*, 65.

41. Dumbrell, "Midian: A Land or a League?," 385.

42. Berlin and Brettler, *Jewish Study Bible*, 110, margin notes for Exod 3:1.

43. Hoffmeier, *Israel in Egypt*, 189.

44. The topic of water in the northern Sinai was discussed with Prof. Haim Gvurtzman in December 2015. Prof. Gvurtzman is a professor of hydrology at the Institute of Earth Sciences at the Hebrew University and a member of the Israel Water Authority Council. He also shared that much of the northern Sinai received its water in the past and in the present from Wadi El Arish, one of the largest wadis in the peninsula.

45. Berlin and Brettler, *Jewish Study Bible*, margin notes on Judg 8:4–9.

46. Davies, *Way of the Wilderness*, 79.

47. Hoffmeier, *Israel in Egypt*, 18.9

48. Hoffmeier, "Search for Migdol of the New Kingdom," 6.

49. Berlin and Brettler, *Jewish Study Bible*, margin notes for Exod 14:2.

50. IPi-hahiroth and Baal-zephon are discussed in Exod 14:2; the first mention of the Sea of Reeds is in 14:9, only a few lines later.

51. In the author's discussions with Prof. Haim Gvurtzman in December 2015, Gvurtzman affirmed that the Bitter Lakes were larger than they are today.

52. In 1995 this author explored this area north of the Wells of Moses and found two small wadis with brackish water and several wells, which produced fresh water from the aquifers in the area.

53. Berlin and Brettler, *Jewish Study Bible*, margin notes for Exod 15:27.

54. Wood, "Tracking the Israelites in Egypt and the Sinai," 14.

55. Palmer, *Exodus and Law Codes in the Torah*, 4.

56. Statement and quote by Hoffmeier are in a presentation titled "Tracking the Israelites in Egypt and the Sinai," sent to the author by Dr. Bryant Wood.

57. Davies, *Way of the Wilderness*, 73.

58. Davies, *Way of the Wilderness*, 73.

59. This group included scholars and archaeologists that are both respected by this writer and considered friends. The group included Dr. Gary Byers, Mr. Walt Pasedag, Mr. Mike Luddeni, and Dr. Bryant G. Wood. Their research and photography were graciously provided to the author by Mike Luddeni and Walt Pasedag.

60. This comment about the restrictions comes from expedition notes provided to this writer by Mike Luddeni and Walt Pasedag.

61. Taken from the first page of notes the Tarif Expedition shared.

62. Berlin and Brettler, *Jewish Study Bible*, margin notes for Exod 3:1.

63. Wood, "What Do Mt. Horeb."

64. Taken from page 3 of the Tarif Expedition notes.

65. Anati, "Gebel Khashm el Tarif."

66. Anati, "Gebel Khashm el Tarif."

67. Jacobovici, *Real Mount Sinai*, 3.

68. Jacobovici, *Real Mount Sinai*, 3.

69. Jacobovici, *Real Mount Sinai*, 3.

70. Quote from page 3 of the Tarif Expedition notes.

71. The date 1440 BCE is provided to give a general time frame and does not presuppose preference over differences in early, late, or middle dating of the exodus.

72. This statement is based on discussions with Prof. Haim Gvirtzman, professor of hydrology at the Institute of Earth Sciences at the Hebrew University and a member of the Israel Water Authority Council. Discussions took place via email and brief telephone conversations in December 2015.

73. Paper provided by Prof. Haim Gvurtzman: El-Bihery, "Groundwater Flow Modeling of Quaternary Aquifer."

74. Wood, "Recent Research," 2.

75. Wood, "Recent Research," 2.

76. Hoffmeier, *Israel in Egypt*, 87.

77. Hoffmeier, *Israel in Egypt*, 109.

78. Collins, *Let My People Go!*, 2.

Endnotes

79. Collins, *Let My People Go!*, 2.

80. Collins, *Let My People Go!*, 5.

81. Rosenberg, "Exodus."

82. Rosenberg, "Exodus."

83. Collins, *Let My People Go!*, 55.

84. Collins, *Let My People Go!*, 55.

Bibliography

Aharoni, Yohanan. *The Land of the Bible: A Historical Geography.* Philadelphia: Westminster, 1979.

Albright, William F. "A Revision of Early Hebrew Chronology." *JPOS* 1 (1920–21) 49–79.

Albright, William F. "From the Patriarchs to Moses." 2 parts. *Biblical Archaeologist* 36/1, 2 (1973) 5–33, 48–76.

Anati, Emmanuel. *The Mountain of God.* New York: Rizzoli, 1986.

———. "Gebel Khashm el Tarif - Ancient Temple in Egypt in Sinai." *The Megalithic Portal*, August 2010. https://www.megalithic.co.uk/article.php?sid=26792.

———. *Is Har Karkom the Biblical Mount Sinai?* Brescia, Italy: Atelier, 2013.

Baly, Denise. *The Geography of the Bible.* New York: Harper & Row, 1974.

Beit-Arieh, Itzhaq. "Fifteen Years in Sinai: Israeli Archaeologists Discover a New World." *Biblical Archaeology Review* 10/4 (1984) 26–54.

———. "The Route Through Sinai: Why the Israelites Fleeing Egypt Went South." *Biblical Archaeology Review* 14/3 (1988) 28–37.

Berlin, Adele, and Marc Zvi Brettler, eds. *The Jewish Study Bible.* Oxford: University, 2004.

Beyerlin, Walter. *Origins and History of the Oldest Sinaitic Traditions.* Translated by Stanley Rudman. Oxford: Blackwell, 1961.

Bietak, Manfred. "Comments on the Exodus." In *Egypt, Israel, Sinai: Archaeological and Historical Relationships in the Biblical Period*, edited by Anson F. Rainey, 163–71. Tel Aviv: Tel Aviv University Press, 1987.

Bimson, John J. *Redating the Exodus and Conquest.* Sheffield: Almond, 1981.

Blum, Howard. *The Gold of Exodus.* New York: Simon & Schuster, 1998.

Bradford, Alfred S. *With Arrow, Sword and Spear: A History of Warfare in the Ancient World.* Westport, CT: Praeger, 2001.

Cassuto, Umberto. *A Commentary on the Book of Exodus.* Jerusalem: Hebrew University Press, 1967.

Childs, Brevard S. *The Book of Exodus: A Critical, Theological Commentary.* Philadelphia: Westminster, 1974.

Cole, R. Alan, *Exodus.* Tyndale Old Testament Commentaries 2. Nottingham: InterVarsity, 1973.

Collins, Steven. *Let My People Go.* Albuquerque, NM: Trinity Southwest University Press, 2005.

Conder, Claude R. *Palestine Exploration Fund Quarterly Statement 1883.* London: Palestine Exploration Fund, 1883.

Coote, Robert B., and Keith W. Whitelam. *The Emergence of Early Israel in Historical Perspective*. Sheffield, UK: Almond, 1987.

Cornuke, Robert, and David Halbrook. *In Search of the Mountain of God: The Discovery of the Real Mt. Sinai*. Nashville: Broadman & Holman, 2000.

Cross, Frank Moore. *Canaanite Myth and Hebrew Epic: Essays in the History of the Religion of Israel*. Cambridge, MA: Harvard University Press, 1973.

Davies, Graham I. *The Way of the Wilderness*. Cambridge: Cambridge University Press, 1979.

De Wit, Constant. *The Date and Route of the Exodus*. London: Tyndale, 1960.

Dever, William G. "Is There any Archaeological Evidence for the Exodus?" In *Exodus: The Egyptian Evidence*, edited by Ernest S. Frerichs et al., 67–86. Winona Lake, IN: Eisenbrauns, 1997.

Dozeman, Thomas B. "The Yam-Sup in the Exodus and the Crossing of the Jordan River." *Catholic Biblical Quarterly* 58/3 (July 1996) 407–16.

Dumbrell, William J. "Midian: A Land or a League?" *Vetus Testamentum* 25 (May 1975) 323–37.

Erman, Adolf. *Life in Ancient Egypt*. London: Macmillan, 1894.

Finkelstein, I., and Neil Asher Silberman. *The Bible Unearthed*. New York: Free Press, 2001.

Fritz, Glen A. *The Lost Sea of the Exodus: A Modern Geographical Analysis*. 2nd ed. San Antonio: GeoTech, 2016.

Gertoux, Gerard. "Moses and the Exodus: Chronological, Historical and Archaeological Evidence." PhD diss., 2015. https://www.academia.edu/14778076/Moses_and_the_Exodus_Chronological_Historical_and_Archaeological_Evidence.

Har-El, Menashe. *The Sinai Journeys: The Route of the Exodus*. San Diego: Ridgefield, 1983

Hobbs, Joseph J. *Mount Sinai*. Austin: University of Texas Press, 1995.

Hoffmeier, James K. *Israel in Egypt*. New York: Oxford University Press, 1996.

Hoffmeier, James K. *The Archaeology of the Bible*. Oxford: Lion Hudson, 2008.

Hoffmeier, James K. "The Search for Migdol of the New Kingdom and Exodus 14:2: An Update." *Buried History* 44 (2008) 3–12. https://www.academia.edu/2015302/The_Search_for_Migdol_of_the_New_Kingdom_and_Exodus_14_2_An_Update_Buried_History_44_2008_3-12.

Jacobovici, Simcha. *The Real Mount Sinai*. Simcha Jacobovici Television, 2013. http://www.simchajtv.com/mount-sinai-found/.

Janzen, Mark. "Ancient Egypt Population Estimates: Slaves and Citizens." *TheTorah.com*, 2016. https://thetorah.com/article/ancient-egypt-population-estimates-slaves-and-citizens.

Kelm, George L. *Escape to Conflict*. Fort Worth: IAR, 1991.

Kitchen, Kenneth A. *On the Reliability of the Old Testament*. Grand Rapids: Eerdmans, 2003.

Levy, Schneider, Thomas Schneider, and William H. C. Propp. *Israel's Exodus in Transdisciplinary Perspective: Text, Archaeology, Culture, and Geoscience*. Cham, Switzerland: Springer, 2015.

MacDonald, Brent. "The Land of Goshen in Egypt." 1999. Lion Tracks Ministries. https://bibleistrue.com/qna/pqna55.htm.

Mariottini, Claude. "Was King Tut the Pharaoh of the Exodus?" Author's blog, April 17, 2014. https://claudemariottini.com/2014/04/17/was-king-tut-the-pharaoh-of-the-exodus/.

Bibliography

Mattfield, Walter. "Various Site Proposals for the Location of Biblical Mount Sinai or Mount Horeb." September 3, 2004. http://www.bibleorigins.net/MountSinaiVariousProposals.html.

Nicholson, Ernest W. *Exodus and Sinai in History and Tradition*. Atlanta: John Knox, 1973.

Noth, Martin, *Exodus: A Commentary*. London: SCM, 1962.

Oblath, Michael D. *The Exodus Itinerary Sites*. New York: Peter Lang, 2004.

Robinson, Edward, and Eli Smith. *Biblical Research in Palestine, Mount Sinai and Arabia Petraea*. Boston: Crocker & Brewster, 1841.

Rosenberg, Stephen G. "The Exodus: Does Archaeology Have a Say?" *Jerusalem Post*, April 14, 2014.

Sawyer, John F. A., and David J. A. Clines. *Midian, Moab and Edom: The History and Archaeology of Late Bronze and Iron Age Jordan and North-West Arabia*, Sheffield, UK: JSOT, 1983.

Schneller, D. Ludwig. *Durch die Wüste zum Sinai: In Moses Spuren vom Schilfmeer bis zum Nebo*. Leipzig: Wallmann, 1910.

Shalom, Paul M., and William G. Dever, eds. *Biblical Archaeology*. Library of Jewish Knowledge. Jerusalem: Keter, 1973.

Todd, William. *New Light on Exodus*. London: Furnival, 1980.

Williams, Larry. *The Mountain of Moses*. New York: Wynwood, 1990.

Wood, Bryant G. "From Ramesses to Shiloh: Archaeological Discoveries Bearing on the Exodus-Judges Period." Associates for Biblical Research, April 2, 2008. https://biblearchaeology.org/research/topics-by-chronology/conquest-of-canaan/2403-from-ramesses-to-shiloh-archaeological-discoveries-bearing-on-the-exodusjudges-period.

———. "Recent Research on the Date and Setting of the Exodus." Associates for Biblical Research, October 19, 2009. https://biblearchaeology.org/research/topics-by-chronology/exodus-era/3288-recent-research-on-the-date-and-setting-of-the-exodus.

———. "Tracking the Israelites in Egypt and the Sinai Part 1: Rameses to Mt. Sinai." Paper presented at the annual meeting of the Near East Archaeological Society, New Orleans, November 18, 2009. Provided by Dr. Wood to the author via email.

———. "What Do Mt. Horeb, The Mountain of God, Mt. Paran and Mt. Seir Have to Do with Mt. Sinai?" Associates for Biblical Research, November 17, 2008. https://biblearchaeology.org/research/topics-by-chronology/exodus-era/4012-what-do-mt-horeb-the-mountain-of-god-mt-paran-and-mt-seir-have-to-do-with-mt-sinai?.

Printed in the USA
CPSIA information can be obtained
at www.ICGtesting.com
LVHW021537210524
780824LV00003B/50